ALL ABOUT THE

USA

A Cultural Reader

SECOND EDITION

Milada Broukal
Peter Murphy

 LONGMAN

Addison Wesley Longman

New York • London • Hong Kong

All About the USA: A Cultural Reader, Second Edition

Addison Wesley Longman, 10 Bank Street, White Plains, NY 10606

Editorial Director: Allen Ascher
Senior acquisitions editor: Louisa Hellegers
Development editors: Nancy Perry/Margaret Grant
Director of design and production: Rhea Banker
Production manager: Marie McNamara
Managing editor: Linda Moser
Associate production editor: Martin Yu
Senior manufacturing supervisor: Patrice Fraccio
Manufacturing supervisor: Edith Pullman
Photo research: Diana Nott
Cover design: Elizabeth Rodrigues
Cover credits: Flag © Bill Howe/Photri; Saxophone © SuperStock,
    Inc.; Statue of Liberty © The Stock Market/Kunio Owaki, 1992;
    White House © George Petrov, Washington Stock Photo, Inc.;
    Baseball © Brian Drake/SportsChrome
Text design adaptation: Rhea Banker
Text art: Pencil Point Studio, except for page 21, Yoshi Miyake;
    page 105, Ron Chironna.
Photo credits: Page 1, From the Collection of The New York
    Historical Society; page 5, UPI/Corbis Bettman; page 9, AP/Wide
    World Photos; page 33, National Park Service: Statue of Liberty
    National Monument; page 37, © The Stock Market/Tibor Bognar, 1992;
    page 41, Photo Courtesy of Washington, DC Convention
    and Visitors Association; page 49, Compliments of The Mall of
    America; page 53, Harriet Beecher Stowe Center, Hartford, CT;
    page 57, John Fitzgerald Kennedy Library; page 61, © Microsoft
    1996; page 69, From the Collections of Henry Ford Museum &
    Greenfield Village; page 89, UPI/Corbis Bettman; page 93, National Baseball
    Hall of Fame Library, Cooperstown, NY; page 101, Library of
    Congress, J.C.H. Grabhill Collection, LC-USZ62-474; page 113,
    National Park Service: Joshua Tree National Park.
Text composition: Publications Development Company

Library of Congress Cataloging-in-Publication Data

Broukal, Milada.
    All about the USA: a cultural reader / Milada Broukal, Peter
Murphy.—2nd ed.
    1. Readers—United States.   2. English language—Textbooks for
foreign speakers.   3. United States—Civilization.   I. Murphy,
Peter.   II. Title.
PE1127.H5B68   1999   99-19385
428.6′4—dc21   CIP

ISBN: 0-201-34673-7

1 2 3 4 5 6 7 8 9 10—ML—04 03 02 01 00 99

CONTENTS

INTRODUCTION

All about the USA is a low-intermediate reader for students of English as a Second Language. A host of facts presented within themes of people, places, originals, food, and nature will not only provide students with information about the United States, but will also stimulate cross-cultural exchange. The vocabulary and structures used in the text have been carefully controlled at a low-intermediate level, and every effort has been made to keep the language natural.

The thirty reading units have been grouped into parts according to their topics to make it easy for teachers to plan sequences of readings on similar themes if they wish.

Each unit contains:

- A prereading activity and introductory visuals
- A short reading passage
- Topic-related vocabulary work
- A comprehension exercise on main ideas
- A comprehension exercise on details
- Grammar exercises
- Discussion questions
- A writing activity

The PREREADING activity focuses the students on the topic of the unit by encouraging speculation about content, involving the students' own experience when possible, and presenting vocabulary as the need arises.

Ideally, students should first read each passage individually, skimming for a general feel for the content. The teacher may wish to deal with some of the vocabulary at this point. A second, more detailed reading can be done while working through the vocabulary exercise. Further reading(s) can be done aloud by the teacher.

The VOCABULARY exercise is designed to help students become more self-reliant by encouraging them to work out the meanings from context. As suggested previously, this section can be done during the reading phase or afterward or both. As in all exercise sections, a variety of exercise types is used.

There are two groups of COMPREHENSION exercises. The first, *Looking for Main Ideas,* should be used in conjunction with the text to help students develop their reading skills, not as a test of memory. In each case, the students are asked to confirm the basic content of the text, which they can do individually, in pairs, in small groups, or as a whole class. The second comprehension exercise, *Looking for Details,* expands the students' exploration of the text, concentrating on the skimming and scanning skills necessary to derive maximum value from reading.

GRAMMAR focuses on aspects of the language suggested by the reading passage itself. The emphasis is on practice and reinforcement of grammar skills rather than teaching; the grammar exercises also indirectly build on the comprehension phase.

DISCUSSION gives students the opportunity to bring their own knowledge and imagination to the topics and related areas. Working in small groups, they may wish to discuss all of the questions or to select one on which to report back to the class.

WRITING provides stimulus for students to write simple sentences or a short paragraph. Teachers should use their own judgment when deciding whether or not to correct the writing exercises.

GEORGE WASHINGTON

Unit 1

PREREADING

Name some famous world leaders.

In 1775, when the American War of Independence began, George Washington was chosen to lead the American army. Washington knew his job would be difficult. The army was small. The soldiers were untrained and had few guns. The British army was large and strong. Its soldiers were very well trained.

The early battles showed Washington's problems. His army was easily defeated in the Battle of New York. Then Washington thought of a plan. On Christmas night in 1776, he had his soldiers attack the enemy in the city of Trenton, New Jersey. The enemy soldiers never expected an attack on such a night. They were having a Christmas party. Washington won his first victory. Washington's army won the final battle in Yorktown in 1781.

George Washington was a great leader and was respected by all his men. He was not interested in fame or money, but only in helping his country. There are many stories about George Washington. Many are probably not true. The most famous story, though, is about the cherry tree. It is said that young George cut down his father's cherry tree. When his father asked who cut down the tree, George confessed and said, "I cannot tell a lie."

In 1789 leaders from all the states met to choose the first president of the United States. The vote was unanimous. Everyone voted for George Washington. He became the country's first president and is remembered as the "Father of our Country."

VOCABULARY

Complete the definitions. Circle the letter of the correct answer.

1. When you admit that you did something wrong, you _____ .
   a. attack
   b. confess
   c. lie

2. When you are beaten, you are _____ .
   a. chosen
   b. voted
   c. defeated

3. When people have a good opinion of someone else, he or she is _____ .
   a. respected
   b. strong
   c. famous

4. When everyone agrees on a decision, the decision is _____ .
   a. large
   b. unanimous
   c. true

5. When you have had no practice doing a job, you are _____ .
   a. not interested
   b. untrained
   c. cut down

6. When two armies fight, it is called a _____ .
   a. party
   b. vote
   c. battle

7. When you are famous or everyone knows you, you have _____ .
   a. fame
   b. money
   c. independence

8. When an army wins, it is called a _____ .
   a. plan
   b. victory
   c. leader

COMPREHENSION

A. Looking for Main Ideas

Write complete answers to these questions.

1. What was George Washington's job during the War of Independence?

   _____

2. Why did people respect George Washington?

   _____

3. What happened to George Washington in 1789?

   _____

B. Looking for Details

Circle T if the sentence is true. Circle F if the sentence is false.

		True	False
1.	George Washington was made president in 1775.	T	F
2.	The British army was bigger than the American army.	T	F
3.	The British soldiers were better trained than the American soldiers.	T	F
4.	The Americans won all their battles.	T	F
5.	The American soldiers had a party at Christmas in Trenton.	T	F
6.	George Washington was not interested in fame or money.	T	F
7.	George Washington cut down his father's cherry tree.	T	F
8.	George Washington was the first president of the United States.	T	F

GRAMMAR

Complete the sentences using the past tense form of the verbs in parentheses.

EXAMPLE: The American War of Independence ___*began*___ in 1775.
                                              (begin)

1. Washington _____ his job would be difficult.
              (know)

2. Washington's army _____ small.
                    (be)

3. The soldiers _____ untrained and _____ few guns.
   (be)   (have)

4. Then Washington _____ of a plan.
   (think)

5. They _____ the enemy on Christmas night.
   (attack)

6. Washington _____ his first victory.
   (win)

7. In 1789 leaders _____ to choose the first president.
   (meet)

8. Everyone _____ for George Washington.
   (vote)

DISCUSSION

Discuss the answers to these questions with your classmates.

1. What other U.S. presidents can you name?

2. What do you know about our present president?

3. What qualities make a great leader?

WRITING

Write six sentences or a short paragraph about a leader of a country. If you write a paragraph, be sure to indent the first sentence.

EXAMPLE: _Margaret Thatcher was the prime minister of England._
She was the first woman to be prime minister.

_____

_____

AMELIA EARHART

PREREADING

Here are some activities that people do even though they are dangerous. Add three other high-risk activities to each list.

Jobs	Sports
deep-sea diver	rock climbing
test pilot	bungee jumping

Amelia Earhart was a famous woman in her time. In 1928, she became the first woman to cross the Atlantic Ocean as a passenger in an airplane. In 1932, she became the first woman pilot to fly solo across the Atlantic. Later that year, she was the first woman to fly across the United States from New Jersey to California. Earhart set records in flying times and won many awards.

Earhart had great courage and ambition. As a child, she was very inquisitive, kind, and always interested in learning. This interest led her to have as many as twenty-eight different jobs in her lifetime. She was a volunteer nurse during World War I. She was an English teacher and social worker at Purdue University in Indiana. She wrote poetry and books and gave many interesting lectures. She encouraged others, especially young women, to follow their dreams.

Amelia Earhart's dream was to fly around the world. Many people gave money to help her. Purdue University gave Earhart her plane. It was the newest type. Earhart began her around-the-world flight on June 1, 1937. Her route around the world was more than 29,000 miles. She had one crew member, Fred Noonan. On July 2, 1937, they were flying over the Pacific when radio contact with her airplane, the *Electra,* suddenly stopped. To this day, no one knows what happened to Amelia Earhart, Fred Noonan, and the *Electra.*

VOCABULARY

Which sentences have the same meaning as the sentences from the reading? Circle the letter of the correct answer.

1. In 1932, Amelia Earhart became the first woman pilot to fly solo across the Atlantic.
   a. She was flying alone.
   b. She was flying with someone else.

2. Earhart set records in flying times.
   a. No one else was flying as fast or as long as Earhart.
   b. Many other people were flying as fast or as long as Earhart.

3. Earhart won many awards.
   a. People gave Earhart many jobs.
   b. People gave Earhart many prizes.

4. Amelia Earhart had great ambition.
   a. She wanted to do many things.
   b. She was very smart.

5. She was very inquisitive.
   a. She studied hard.
   b. She asked many questions.

6. She was a social worker at Purdue University.
   a. She was teaching history.
   b. She was helping people.

7. She encouraged others to follow their dreams.
   a. She thanked people for doing what they wanted to do.
   b. She told people to go and do the things they wanted to do.

8. She had one crew member, Fred Noonan.
   a. Fred Noonan helped Amelia Earhart fly her plane.
   b. Amelia Earhart gave Fred Noonan a ride in her plane.

COMPREHENSION

A. Looking for Main Ideas

Write complete answers to these questions.

1. Why was Amelia Earhart famous in her time?

   _____ .

2. What kind of woman was Amelia Earhart?

   _____ .

3. Why is Amelia Earhart's last flight a mystery?

   _____ .

B. Looking for Details

Circle the letter of the best answer.

1. Amelia Earhart disappeared while she was flying _____ .
   a. solo across the Atlantic
   b. from New Jersey to California
   c. her plane around the world

2. In 1928, Amelia Earhart became _____ .
   a. the first woman pilot
   b. the first woman to cross the Atlantic as a passenger in an airplane
   c. the first woman to fly from the East Coast to the West Coast

3. As a child, Amelia Earhart was always interested in _____ .
   a. flying
   b. learning
   c. teaching

4. _____ , Amelia Earhart worked as a nurse.
   a. While she was at Purdue University
   b. After she learned to fly a plane
   c. During World War I

5. Earhart's dream was to _____ .
   a. fly around the world
   b. build a modern airplane
   c. teach young women how to fly

6. _____ gave Earhart the *Electra*.
   a. Purdue University
   b. Fred Noonan
   c. Several wealthy people

GRAMMAR

Complete the sentences with the correct article. Use _a_ or _the._ If no article is necessary, write _X._

1. Amelia Earhart was _____ famous woman in her time.

2. In 1928, she became _____ first woman to cross _____ Atlantic Ocean as _____ passenger in an airplane.

3. She was _____ first woman to fly across _____ United States from _____ New Jersey to _____ California.

4. She won many _____ awards.

5. She was _____ volunteer nurse.

6. She wrote _____ poetry and _____ books.

7. Many people gave _____ money to help her.

8. Her route around _____ world was more than 29,000 miles.

DISCUSSION

Discuss the answers to these questions with your classmates.

1. Do you like to fly in airplanes? Why or why not?

2. What do you think happened to Amelia Earhart?

3. Some people have dangerous jobs. Others like to play dangerous sports. What are some of the reasons that people risk their lives?

WRITING

Write six sentences or a short paragraph about your dream in life. If you write a paragraph, be sure to indent the first sentence.

EXAMPLE: _My dream in life is to become a nurse. I have wanted to be a nurse since I was a child._

_____

_____

JESSE OWENS

PREREADING

Name some famous people in sports. Then say what sports they are famous for.

Name	Sport
Muhammad Ali	boxing

Jesse Owens was born in Alabama in 1913 to a poor, black family. Even when Owens was a boy, it was clear that he had special athletic ability. He could run extremely fast. In high school he was a long-jump champion.

Owen's family didn't have enough money to send him to college. However, because he was an excellent athlete, he was able to get a scholarship to Ohio State University. Owens was the star of the Ohio State track team. In one college track event in 1935, he broke three world records in less than an hour! Owens was chosen for the 1936 U.S. Olympic team.

The 1936 Summer Olympics were held in Berlin, Germany. Adolf Hitler had come to power two years before. Hitler believed that the people of Germany and other northern European countries were better than all other people in the world. Hitler wanted to show the world the Germans were the best so he ordered the German team to train hard.

At the Olympics, Jesse Owens won both the 100-meter race and the 200-meter race. His time in the 200-meter race set a new Olympic record. Owens was also on the U.S. 400-meter relay team. The U.S. relay team won.

Then came the long jump. A German athlete broke the Olympic record. Hitler said that he personally would congratulate the winner. But Owens still had one more jump. He jumped several inches farther than the German athlete. Hitler left the stadium in anger. Jesse Owens, a black American, had won his fourth gold medal at the Olympics. Jesse Owens was a hero.

VOCABULARY

Complete the sentences. Circle the letter of the correct answer.

1. Jesse Owens got a _____ to Ohio State University.
   a. record   **b.** scholarship   **c.** champion

2. Jesse Owens was the star of the Ohio State _____ team.
   a. country   **b.** meter   **c.** track

3. The 1936 Olympics were _____ in Berlin.
   a. left   **b.** held   **c.** chosen

4. Hitler ordered the German team to _____ hard.
   a. train   **b.** relay   **c.** win

5. Jesse Owens jumped several inches _____ than the German athlete.
   a. faster   **b.** farther   **c.** lower

6. The U.S. _____ team won.
   a. jump   **b.** gold   **c.** relay

7. In the 200-meter race, Owens _____ a new Olympic record.
   a. chose   **b.** set   **c.** won

8. Hitler left the _____ in anger.
   a. American   **b.** team   **c.** stadium

COMPREHENSION

A. Looking for Main Ideas

Write complete answers to these questions.

1. What special ability did Jesse Owens have?

   _____

2. What did Hitler want to show the world?

   _____

3. How many gold medals did Owens win at the 1936 Olympics?

   _____

B. Looking for Details

Number the sentences 1 through 8 to show the correct order.

_____ He went to Ohio State University.

_____ He went to Berlin in 1936.

_____ Jesse Owens was born in Alabama in 1913.

_____ He was a long-jump champion in high school.

_____ He set an Olympic record for the 200-meter race.

_____ Jesse Owens won the 100- and 200-meter races.

_____ He was chosen for the U.S. Olympic team.

_____ He then won the long jump by several inches.

GRAMMAR

Complete the sentences with the correct article. Use _a_, _an_, or _the_. If no article is necessary, write _X_.

EXAMPLE: Hitler ordered __the__ German team to train hard.

1. Jesse Owens was born in _____ Alabama.

2. He got _____ scholarship to _____ Ohio State University.

3. Owens was chosen for _____ 1936 U.S. Olympic team.

4. Owens was _____ excellent athlete.

5. Hitler wanted to show _____ world _____ Germans were _____ best.

6. Hitler said he would congratulate _____ winner.

7. Jesse Owens won his fourth gold medal at _____ Olympics.

8. Jesse Owens was _____ hero.

DISCUSSION

Discuss the answers to these questions with your classmates.

1. What other athletes have won Olympic medals?

2. Do you think athletes should be paid to participate in the Olympics?

3. What Olympic events do you like best? Why?

WRITING

Write six sentences or a short paragraph about a famous sports person. If you write a paragraph, be sure to indent the first sentence.

EXAMPLE: _Muhammad Ali is a famous boxer. His original name was_

Cassius Clay.

_____

_____

ALEXANDER GRAHAM BELL

Unit 4

PREREADING

Name some famous inventions that have changed our lives.

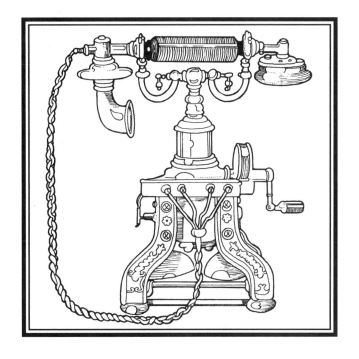

Alexander Graham Bell was born in 1847 in Edinburgh, Scotland. His father was an expert in phonetics, the study of the sounds of languages. As a boy, Bell became interested in sounds and speech.

In 1870 the Bells decided to emigrate to America. They lived in Boston, where Alexander taught in a school for the deaf. There he began experimenting with a machine to help the deaf hear.

While experimenting with this machine, Bell had an idea. Why not use electricity to send the human voice from one place to another? Bell began work on a new invention.

For years Bell and his assistant, Thomas Watson, worked day and night. They rented rooms in a boardinghouse. Bell was on one floor, and Watson was on another. They tried to send speech through a wire. Finally, on March 19, 1876, Watson heard these words very clearly: "Mr. Watson, come here. I want you." Watson rushed upstairs, ran into Bell's room, and shouted, "I heard you!"

That year was the centennial, or 100th birthday, of the United States. There was a large fair in Philadelphia, called the Centennial Exposition. One of the main attractions at the exposition was Bell's "talking machine." Thousands of visitors, including Don Pedro, the emperor of Brazil, were surprised when they saw—and heard—this invention. But they still thought it was just an interesting toy. They didn't know that one day this talking machine would become the telephone and would change people's lives.

VOCABULARY

Replace the underlined words in the sentences with the words below.

an expert	boardinghouse	the deaf	wire
fair	experiment	attractions	rushed

1. Alexander Graham Bell taught in a school for <u>people who cannot hear</u>.

2. Watson and Bell tried to send speech through a <u>thin piece of metal</u>.

3. In Philadelphia there was a large <u>show where people see new things</u> called the Centennial Exposition.

4. Bell's father was <u>a person who knew a lot about and had training</u> in phonetics.

5. Bell and Watson stayed in a <u>house where there were many rooms to rent</u>.

6. Bell began to <u>try new ideas</u> with a machine to help people who could not hear.

7. One of the <u>interesting things to see</u> at the Centennial Exposition was Bell's "talking machine."

8. When he heard the words, Watson <u>went quickly</u> upstairs, ran into Bell's room, and shouted, "I heard you!"

COMPREHENSION

A. Looking for Main Ideas

Circle the letter of the best answer.

1. As a boy, Bell was interested in sounds and speech because _____ .
   a. he studied phonetics
   b. his father was an expert in phonetics
   c. he was born in Scotland

2. Bell and his assistant Watson _____ .

    a. liked to live in a boardinghouse

    b. could not hear very clearly

    c. tried to send speech through a wire

3. _____ was one of the main attractions at the Centennial Exposition.

    a. Bell's "talking machine"

    b. Don Pedro, the emperor of Brazil

    c. The large fair

B. Looking for Details

Circle T if the sentence is true. Circle F if the sentence is false.

		True	False
1.	Alexander Graham Bell taught in a school for the deaf in Boston.	T	F
2.	Bell and Watson worked together for years.	T	F
3.	Bell and Watson were on the same floor in the boardinghouse in Boston.	T	F
4.	Bell rushed upstairs and shouted, "I heard you!"	T	F
5.	Don Pedro, the emperor of Brazil, was surprised when he saw the thousands of visitors.	T	F
6.	Alexander Graham Bell came to America in 1870.	T	F

GRAMMAR

Complete the sentences with the prepositions below.

through	on	from	in	to

EXAMPLE: Alexander Graham Bell was born _____in_____ Scotland.

1. Bell's father was an expert _____ phonetics.

2. The Bells emigrated _____ America.

3. Bell taught _____ a school for the deaf.

4. Bell was _____ one floor and Watson was _____ another.

5. Bell and Watson tried to send speech _____ a wire.

6. Bell used electricity to send the human voice _____ one place _____ another.

DISCUSSION

Discuss the answers to these questions with your classmates.

1. How do you think the invention of the telephone changed people's lives?

2. How do you think the telephone will change in the future?

3. What kind of invention would you like to work on?

WRITING

Write six sentences or a short paragraph about an invention that has changed our lives. If you write a paragraph, be sure to indent the first sentence.

EXAMPLE: _Television has changed our lives in good ways and bad._

Before television, we did not get the news instantly.

_____

_____

Unit 5 • THANKSGIVING
Unit 6 • BODY LANGUAGE
Unit 7 • BLUE JEANS
Unit 8 • THE AMERICAN COWBOY

THANKSGIVING

Unit 5

PREREADING

Check the things you think are associated with Thanksgiving.

_____ **1.** turkey

_____ **2.** cranberry sauce

_____ **3.** a large family meal

_____ **4.** greeting cards

_____ **5.** fish

_____ **6.** pumpkin pie

_____ **7.** giving gifts

_____ **8.** costumes

On the fourth Thursday in November, in houses around the United States, families get together for a feast, or a large meal. Almost all families eat turkey and cranberry sauce for this meal, and have pumpkin pie for dessert. This feast is part of a very special day, the holiday of Thanksgiving.

In 1620 the Pilgrims made a difficult trip across the ocean from England. They landed in what is now Massachusetts. In England the Pilgrims had not been allowed to freely practice their religion. So they went to the New World in search of religious freedom.

The Pilgrims' first winter was very hard. Almost half the group died of cold, hunger, and disease. But the Native Americans of Massachusetts taught the Pilgrims to plant corn, to hunt, and to fish. When the next fall came, the Pilgrims had plenty of food. They were thankful and had a feast to give thanks. They invited the Native Americans to join them. This was the first Thanksgiving.

Thanksgiving became a national holiday many years later because of a woman named Sarah Hale. For forty years Sarah Hale wrote to each president and asked for a holiday of Thanksgiving. At last she was successful. In 1863 President Lincoln declared Thanksgiving a holiday.

How much is Thanksgiving today like the Pilgrims' Thanksgiving? In many ways they are different. For example, historians think that the Pilgrims ate deer, not turkey. The idea of Thanksgiving, though, is very much the same: Thanksgiving is a day on which we celebrate and give thanks.

VOCABULARY

Complete the definitions. Circle the letter of the correct answer.

1. The last part of a meal is called the _____ .
   a. breakfast   **b.** dessert   **c.** lunch

2. When a boat or an airplane has arrived from somewhere we say it has _____ .
   a. feasted   **b.** joined   **c.** landed

3. People who travel from one place to another for religious reasons are _____ .
   a. pilgrims   **b.** families   **c.** Native Americans

4. When you are sick, you may have a _____ .
   a. hunger   **b.** feast   **c.** disease

5. When you look for animals to kill for food, you _____ .
   a. plant   **b.** hunt   **c.** eat

6. When you have more than you need, you have _____ .
   a. much   **b.** half   **c.** plenty

7. When the government of a country decides to celebrate a special day, it _____ a holiday.

    a. declares   **b.** asks for   **c.** invites

8. People who write history are called _____ .

    a. religious   **b.** historians   **c.** turkeys

COMPREHENSION

A. Looking for Main Ideas

Write the questions for these answers.

1. When _____ ?
Thanksgiving is celebrated on the fourth Thursday in November.

2. Who _____ ?
The Pilgrims were religious people from England.

3. Why _____ ?
They were thankful for food after a hard winter.

B. Looking for Details

Number the sentences 1 through 8 to show the correct order.

_____ The Native Americans taught the Pilgrims to hunt and plant corn.

_____ In 1863 President Lincoln declared Thanksgiving a holiday.

_____ The Pilgrims left England in search of religious freedom.

_____ Sarah Hale asked every president to make Thanksgiving a national holiday.

_____ In 1620 the Pilgrims landed in Massachusetts.

_____ The Pilgrims invited the Native Americans to the first Thanksgiving.

_____ The Pilgrims' first winter was hard.

_____ Today, Thanksgiving is a day on which we give thanks.

GRAMMAR

Complete the sentences using the past tense form of the verbs in parentheses.

EXAMPLE: The Native Americans ___taught___ the Pilgrims to fish.
(teach)

1. The Pilgrims _____ in Massachusetts.
   (land)

2. The first winter _____ hard for the Pilgrims.
   (be)

3. Almost half the Pilgrims _____ during the first winter.
   (die)

4. In the fall, the Pilgrims _____ plenty of food.
   (have)

5. The Native Americans _____ the Pilgrims to plant corn.
   (teach)

6. The Pilgrims _____ the Native Americans to join them for a feast.
   (invite)

DISCUSSION

Discuss the answers to these questions with your classmates.

1. What other American holidays do you know?

2. What holidays do you have in your country that are not celebrated in the United States?

WRITING

Write a short paragraph about how you celebrate a holiday in your country. Be sure to indent the first sentence.

EXAMPLE: ___In Mexico, on November 2 we celebrate the Day of the___
___Dead. We prepare for this special day in advance.___

_____

_____

BODY LANGUAGE

Unit 6

PREREADING

What gestures do you use in your country to do the things listed below? Add three more gestures to the list.

To	We do this
say goodbye	Example: *wave a hand up and down*
call someone to us	
show we don't like something	
show we don't believe something	
show we are confused	
show we have no money	
show we are becoming impatient	

Sometimes people add to what they say even when they don't talk. Gestures are the "silent language" of every culture. We point a finger or move another part of the body to show what we want to say. It is important to know the body language of every country or we may be misunderstood.

In the United States, people greet each other with a handshake in a formal introduction. The handshake must be firm. If the handshake is weak, it is a sign of weakness or unfriendliness. Friends may place a hand on the

other's arm or shoulder. Some people, usually women, greet a friend with a hug.

Space is important to Americans. When two people talk to each other, they stand two and a half feet away at an angle, so they are not facing each other directly. Americans get uncomfortable when a person stands too close. They will move back to have their space. If Americans touch another person by accident, they say, "Pardon me," or "Excuse me."

Americans like to look the other person in the eyes when they are talking. If you don't do so, it means you are bored, hiding something, or are not interested. But when you stare at someone, it is not polite.

For Americans, thumbs up means yes, very good, or well done. Thumbs down means the opposite. To call a waiter, raise one hand to head level or above. To show you want the check, make a movement with your hands as if you are signing a piece of paper. It is all right to point at things but not at people with the hand and index finger. Americans shake their index finger at children when they scold them and pat them on the head when they admire them.

Learning a culture's body language is sometimes confusing. If you don't know what to do, the safest thing to do is to smile.

VOCABULARY

What is the meaning of the underlined words? Circle the letter of the correct answer.

1. People greet each other with a handshake in a <u>formal</u> introduction.
   a. in a different or imaginative way
   b. according to a certain custom or rule

2. The handshake must be <u>firm</u>.
   a. strong and hard
   b. fast and loose

3. Some people greet a friend with a <u>hug</u>.
   a. putting your hands on a person's shoulders
   b. putting your arms around a person

4. They stand two and a half feet away at an <u>angle</u>.
   a. turned to the side
   b. facing straight ahead

5. But when you <u>stare at</u> someone it is not polite.
   a. to look at for a long time
   b. to look at quickly

6. It is all right to point at things with the hand and <u>index finger</u>.
   a. the middle finger
   b. the finger next to the thumb

7. Americans shake their index finger at children when they <u>scold</u> them.

   a. call them to their side

   b. tell them they are doing something wrong

8. They <u>pat</u> them on the head when they admire them.

   a. touch lightly with the hand

   b. move the hand across the head to remove the hair

COMPREHENSION

A. Looking for Main Ideas

Write complete answers to these questions.

1. What do people use to say more when they don't talk at all?

_____ .

2. Why is it important to know the body language of a country?

_____ .

3. Why must a person not stand too close while talking to an American?

_____ .

B. Looking for Details

Circle the letter of the best answer.

1. In a formal introduction, Americans greet each other _____ .

   a. with a hug

   b. with a handshake

   c. by placing a hand on each other's arm

2. When Americans talk to each other, they do not _____ .

   a. face each other directly

   b. talk loudly

   c. look at each other directly

3. Americans feel uncomfortable when a person _____ .

   a. points with the index finger

   b. stands too close

   c. looks them in the eyes

4. In the United States, if a person touches another by accident, they _____ .

   a. move away

   b. stare at each other

   c. say, "Excuse me."

GRAMMAR

Complete the sentences with the prepositions below.

by	in	with	at	of	on

EXAMPLE: Gestures are the "silent language" ___*of*___ every culture.

1. We move a part _____ the body to show what we want to say.

2. In the United States, people greet each other _____ a handshake.

3. Friends may place a hand _____ each other's arm.

4. Americans say "Pardon me" if they touch someone _____ accident.

5. When they are talking, Americans like to look the other person _____ the eyes.

6. When you stare _____ someone, it is not polite.

DISCUSSION

Discuss the answers to these questions with your classmates.

1. What American customs seem strange to you?

2. What are the rules about greeting people in your country? When do you shake hands? When do you kiss? How do you say goodbye?

3. Give two examples of bad manners in your country. For example, in the United States it is not polite to ask a person how much he or she earns.

WRITING

Write six sentences or a short paragraph about what advice you would give someone coming to live and work in your country. If you write a paragraph, be sure to indent the first sentence.

EXAMPLE: In Japan, we have strict rules about business behavior. You must exchange business cards immediately when you meet. You must read the card, but you should not put it in your pocket.

BLUE JEANS

Unit 7

PREREADING

What do you know about the history of blue jeans? Circle T or F.

		True	False
1.	Levi Strauss was the first person to make blue jeans.	T	F
2.	Levi Strauss was born in the United States.	T	F
3.	Strauss got the idea to make jeans from an American woman.	T	F
4.	Strauss made his first jeans from canvas for tents.	T	F
5.	The first jeans were not blue.	T	F
6.	Cowboys wore the first jeans.	T	F

Levi Strauss, a young immigrant from Germany, arrived in San Francisco in 1850. California was in the middle of the Gold Rush. Thousands of men were coming to California to dig for gold. And Strauss came to sell canvas to these gold miners. Canvas is a heavy fabric. So Strauss thought the miners could use the canvas for tents.

One day Strauss heard a miner complain that he couldn't find clothes strong enough for the work he was doing. Strauss got an idea. He quickly took some of his canvas and made it into pants. These pants were what the miners needed. In one day Strauss sold all the pants he had made.

Strauss wanted to improve his pants. He wanted to make them even better. He bought a fabric that was softer than canvas but just as strong. This fabric came from Nîmes, a city in France, and was called *serge de Nîmes.* The miners liked this fabric. They called it "denim" (from *de Nîmes*) and bought even more pants from Strauss.

However, denim had no color. Because of this the denim pants did not look very interesting, and they got dirty easily. To solve these problems, Strauss dyed the denim blue.

Strauss continued to improve his jeans. Today, the company he started is known around the world. And jeans are considered not just practical but very fashionable as well.

VOCABULARY

What is the meaning of the underlined words? Circle the letter of the correct answer.

1. Strauss was a young underline{immigrant}.
    a. person who moves to another country
    b. person who is good in business

2. Canvas is a heavy fabric.
    a. machine
    b. cloth

3. The miners complained that they didn't have strong clothes.
    a. told about problems
    b. told stories

4. Strauss wanted to improve his pants.
    a. make them better
    b. make them cleaner

5. Strauss dyed the denim.
    a. changed the texture
    b. changed the color

6. Today, jeans are considered good for many uses.
    a. thought to be
    b. made to be

7. Blue jeans are <u>practical</u>.

    a. cheap

    b. useful

8. Blue jeans are <u>fashionable</u>.

    a. popular to wear

    b. interesting

COMPREHENSION

A. Looking for Main Ideas

Write complete answers to these questions.

1. Why did Levi Strauss come to California?

_____

2. What did the miners need?

_____

3. How did Strauss improve his pants?

_____

B. Looking for Details

***One* word in each sentence is *not* correct. Cross out the word and write the correct answer above it.**

1. Levi Strauss came to Germany in 1850.

2. There were thousands of men digging for canvas.

3. Levi Strauss came to buy canvas.

4. The miners needed clean pants.

5. Strauss made tents from denim.

6. Strauss got the denim from Germany.

7. Strauss dyed the denim red.

8. Levi jeans are known all over the United States.

GRAMMAR

Replace the underlined pronouns in the sentences with the correct nouns.

canvas	Miners	Levi Strauss	pants	the denim

1. <u>They</u> came to California for gold.

2. <u>He</u> came to California to sell canvas.

3. Miners used <u>it</u> to make tents.

4. Strauss used canvas to make <u>them</u>.

5. He dyed <u>it</u> blue.

6. Miners came to <u>him</u> to buy blue jeans.

DISCUSSION

Discuss the answers to these questions with your classmates.

1. Do you think Levi Strauss was a good businessman? Why or why not? Are you good in business?

2. If you could have your own business, what would it be?

3. What can clothes tell you about people?

WRITING

Write six sentences or a short paragraph about what you like to wear at home or at school. If you write a paragraph, be sure to indent the first sentence.

EXAMPLE: _At home I like to wear comfortable clothes. I usually wear jeans._

THE AMERICAN COWBOY

Unit 8

PREREADING

Check the characteristics you think are associated with cowboys.

_____ **1.** moving from place to place

_____ **2.** being free

_____ **3.** being married

_____ **4.** having many friends

_____ **5.** being sensitive

_____ **6.** fighting for what is right

_____ **7.** being good with a gun

The cowboy is the hero of many movies. He is, even today, a symbol of courage and adventure. But what was the life of the cowboy really like?

The cowboy's job is clear from the word *cowboy.* Cowboys were men who took care of cows and other cattle. The cattle were in the West and in Texas. People in the cities of the East wanted beef from these cattle. Trains could take the cattle east. But first the cattle had to get to the trains. Part of the cowboy's job was to take the cattle hundreds of miles to the railroad towns.

The trips were called *cattle drives.* A cattle drive usually took several months. Cowboys rode for sixteen hours a day. Because they rode so much, each cowboy brought along about eight horses. A cowboy changed horses several times each day.

The cowboys had to make sure that the cattle arrived safely. Before starting on a drive, the cowboys branded the cattle. They burned a mark on the cattle to show who they belonged to. But these marks didn't stop rustlers, or cattle thieves. Cowboys had to protect the cattle from rustlers. Rustlers made the dangerous trip even more dangerous.

Even though their work was very difficult and dangerous, cowboys did not earn much money. They were paid badly. Yet cowboys liked their way of life. They lived in a wild and open country. They lived a life of adventure and freedom.

VOCABULARY

Complete the definitions. Circle the letter of the correct answer.

1. Cows are a type of _____ .
   a. cowboy　　　　**b.** cattle　　　　**c.** drive

2. When cowboys take a group of cows from one place to another it is called a cattle _____ .
   a. drive　　　　**b.** trip　　　　**c.** train

3. People who steal cattle are _____ .
   a. cows　　　　**b.** marks　　　　**c.** rustlers

4. When cowboys burned a mark into the cattle, they _____ .
   a. rode them　　　　**b.** branded them　　　　**c.** drove them

5. The cowboy was the most important person in the movie. He was the _____ .
   a. chief　　　　**b.** rustler　　　　**c.** hero

6. The action of taking things or people with you is _____ .
   a. taking care of　　　　**b.** bringing along　　　　**c.** getting to

7. When you are not afraid to do something, you have _____ .
   a. freedom　　　　**b.** courage　　　　**c.** life

8. When you do something new and exciting, you have _____ .
   a. a symbol　　　　**b.** an adventure　　　　**c.** a job

COMPREHENSION

A. Looking for Main Ideas

Circle the letter of the best answer.

1. A cowboy is _____ .
   - **a.** a symbol of courage and adventure
   - **b.** not really a symbol
   - **c.** a symbol of movies

2. The cowboy's job was to _____ .
   - **a.** be a hero
   - **b.** take care of cattle
   - **c.** be a rustler

3. Cowboys _____ .
   - **a.** made a lot of money
   - **b.** had a difficult job
   - **c.** did not like their way of life

B. Looking for Details

One word in each sentence is *not* correct. Cross out the word and write the correct answer above It.

1. Trains took the cattle west.

2. Cowboys rode for eight hours a day.

3. Each cowboy brought along about sixteen horses.

4. A cattle drive took several days.

5. The cowboys burned a mark on the rustlers.

6. The cowboys had to protect the rustlers.

7. People in the East wanted cowboys.

8. Cowboys were paid well.

GRAMMAR

Complete the sentences with the correct article. Use *the* or *a.* If no article is necessary, write *X.*

EXAMPLE: _The_ cowboy is _the_ hero of many movies.

1. The cowboy is _____ symbol of courage and adventure.

2. The cattle were in _____ West and in _____ Texas.

3. People in _____ cities of _____ East wanted _____ beef.

4. The cowboy's job is clear from _____ word *cowboy.*

5. Cowboys rode for sixteen hours _____ day.

6. Each cowboy brought along about _____ eight horses.

7. Cowboys burned _____ mark on the cattle to show who they belonged to.

8. Cowboys lived a life of _____ adventure.

DISCUSSION

Discuss the answers to these questions with your classmates.

1. What qualities do male heroes in movies and TV shows in your country have?

2. We often see cowboys and images of the old West in advertisements of American products such as cigarettes, trucks, and blue jeans. Why do you think advertisers use cowboys to sell these products?

3. What is your impression of a cowboy's life? Would you like to live the life of a cowboy?

WRITING

Write six sentences or a short paragraph about a TV or movie hero. If you write a paragraph, be sure to indent the first sentence.

EXAMPLE: _I like Jackie Chan. He is my hero. In his movies, he. . . ._

_____

_____

THE STATUE OF LIBERTY

Unit 9

PREREADING

Name some statues, buildings, monuments, mountains, or other features associated with certain cities.

City	Statue/Monument
Moscow	St. Basil's Cathedral

One of the most famous statues in the world stands on an island in New York Harbor. This statue is, of course, the Statue of Liberty. The Statue of Liberty is a woman who holds a torch up high. Visitors can go inside the statue. The statue is so large that as many as twelve people can stand inside the torch. Many more people can stand in other parts of the statue. The statue weighs 225 tons and is 301 feet tall.

The Statue of Liberty was put up in 1886. It was a gift to the

United States from the people of France. Over the years France and the United States had a special relationship. In 1776 France helped the American colonies gain independence from England. The French wanted to do something special for the U.S. centennial, its 100th birthday.

Laboulaye was a well-known Frenchman who admired the United States. One night at a dinner in his house, Laboulaye talked about the idea of a gift. Among Laboulaye's guests was the French sculptor Frédéric-Auguste Bartholdi. Bartholdi thought of a statue of liberty. He offered to design the statue.

Many people contributed in some way. The French people gave money for the statue. Americans designed and built the pedestal for the statue to stand on. The American people raised money to pay for the pedestal. The French engineer Alexandre Eiffel, who was famous for his Eiffel Tower in Paris, figured out how to make the heavy statue stand.

In the years after the statue was put up, many immigrants came to the United States through New York. As they entered New York Harbor, they saw the Statue of Liberty holding up her torch. She symbolized a welcome to a land of freedom.

VOCABULARY

Complete the sentences. Circle the letter of the correct answer.

1. The people of France wanted to give the United States a special _____ .
   a. gift
   b. torch

2. France and the United States had a special _____ .
   a. independence
   b. relationship

3. France helped the American colonies _____ independence.
   a. build
   b. gain

4. A famous Frenchman, Laboulaye, _____ the United States.
   a. admired
   b. visited

5. Frédéric-Auguste Bartholdi _____ to design the statue.
   a. contributed
   b. offered

6. The Statue of Liberty stands on a _____ .
   a. pedestal
   b. harbor

COMPREHENSION

A. Looking for Main Ideas

Circle the letter of the best answer.

1. The Statue of Liberty is a famous statue in _____ .
   a. France
   b. the United States

2. The Statue of Liberty was a gift from _____ .
   a. the people of France to the United States
   b. Laboulaye and Eiffel to the United States

3. The Statue of Liberty symbolizes a _____ .
   a. woman with a torch
   b. land of freedom

B. Looking for Details

Circle T if the sentence is true. Circle F if the sentence is false.

	True	False
1. Twelve people can stand inside the torch of the Statue of Liberty.	T	F
2. The United States helped France gain its independence in 1776.	T	F
3. Alexandre Eiffel was among the guests at Laboulaye's house.	T	F
4. Frédéric-Auguste Bartholdi was a French engineer.	T	F
5. Alexandre Eiffel figured out how to make the statue stand.	T	F
6. Americans designed the pedestal for the statue.	T	F

GRAMMAR

Complete the sentences with the correct article. Use _a_ or _the_. If no article is necessary, write _X_.

EXAMPLE: __The__ statue stands on an island in _____X_____ New York Harbor.

1. _____ Statue of _____ Liberty was _____ gift to _____ United States

   from _____ people of _____ France.

2. Over _____ years _____ France and _____ United States had _____

   special relationship.

3. In _____ 1776 _____ France helped _____ American colonies gain _____ independence from _____ England.

4. _____ French paid for _____ statue.

5. _____ American people paid for _____ pedestal.

DISCUSSION

Discuss the answers to these questions with your classmates.

1. Do you have any famous statues or monuments in your country? What are they?

2. What famous statue, monument, or building do you think is the most beautiful or interesting? Which do you think is the ugliest?

WRITING

Write six sentences or a short paragraph about a statue, monument, or building. If you write a paragraph, be sure to indent the first sentence.

EXAMPLE: The pyramids in Egypt are very interesting monuments. The pharoahs of Egypt had the pyramids built more than 5,000 years ago.

LAS VEGAS

PREREADING

Some people associate certain cities with certain things. Name other cities and what you associate with them.

City	Association
Paris	romance
New York	skyscrapers

Las Vegas, Nevada, is the most famous city for gambling in the United States. Some people say that Las Vegas is a mispronunciation of "lost wages." The casinos and hotels have so many neon lights that some people call this city in the desert "The City of Lights."

Each of the big hotels in Las Vegas is special. Going into one is like entering another world. One hotel is like ancient Egypt. Another is like a tropical island. Still another is like New York City. These hotels have shows with famous entertainers. Everything looks expensive. But the rooms cost half the price of rooms in other places. And the restaurants have all-you-can-eat meals for very little money. That's because the hotels make their money from the gambling casinos.

Las Vegas started in 1905 as a small train stop. There were only a few buildings in the middle of the desert. In 1946, a famous gangster named Bugsy Siegel built the first casino. He was murdered in 1947. This made him and Las Vegas more famous! In the early 1950s, tourists went to Las Vegas not only to gamble. They went to watch atomic bomb tests in the desert outside the city. In those days, people didn't know it was dangerous. They thought it was exciting.

Las Vegas is also famous for its many wedding chapels. Like all of Las Vegas, they are open twenty-four hours a day. Getting married is easy. A couple just pays a few dollars for a license, and they can get married immediately. They don't have to wait. Many famous movie stars were married in Las Vegas.

It is interesting that Las Vegas has more churches for its population than anywhere else in the United States. That's not counting wedding chapels. Another interesting fact is that tourists have a greater chance of having a heart attack in Las Vegas than in any other American city.

VOCABULARY

Complete the sentences with one of the following words.

chapels	gambling	license	Casinos
gangster	mispronunciation	Neon	couple

1. A person who belongs to a group of criminals is a _____ .

2. If you play a game to win money, you are _____ .

3. Two people who are married, engaged, or dating are a _____ .

4. _____ is a gas that is used in certain lights.

5. An official paper or card that gives permission to do something is

   a _____ .

6. _____ are buildings or rooms used for playing games to win money.

7. Making a mistake in how you say a word is a _____ .

8. Rooms or small buildings used for marriage, funeral, or other religious services

   are _____ .

COMPREHENSION

A. Looking for Main Ideas

Write complete answers to these questions.

1. What is special about the hotels in Las Vegas?

   _____.

2. Why is Las Vegas called the "City of Lights?"

   _____.

3. What does Las Vegas have that other cities don't have?

   _____.

B. Looking for Details

Circle T if the sentence is true. Circle F if the sentence is false.

	True	False
1. Some people think Las Vegas means "Lost Desert."	T	F
2. Las Vegas started as a farming town.	T	F
3. It costs a lot of money to stay in a hotel in Las Vegas.	T	F
4. A gangster named Bugsy Siegel built the first casino in Las Vegas.	T	F
5. No one wanted to go to Las Vegas after Bugsy Siegel was murdered.	T	F
6. It is easy to get married in Las Vegas.	T	F
7. In the 1950s, tourists went to Las Vegas to see atomic bomb tests.	T	F

GRAMMAR

Complete the sentences with the prepositions below.

in	for	of	with	from	to

EXAMPLE: There are many hotels _____in_____ Las Vegas.

1. Las Vegas is a place _____ gambling.

2. Many people go to Las Vegas to see shows _____ famous entertainers.

3. The casinos make a lot of money _____ tourists who gamble.

4. Bugsy Siegel was murdered _____ 1947.

5. Many famous movie stars go _____ Las Vegas to get married.

6. The chance _____ having a heart attack in Las Vegas is greater than in any other American city.

DISCUSSION

Discuss the answers to these questions with your classmates.

1. Certain cities do not allow gambling. Do you think this is a good idea? Why or why not?

2. Some people like to go to Las Vegas. Where would you like to go for fun? Why?

3. Why do you think tourists have a greater chance of having a heart attack in Las Vegas than in any other city in the United States?

WRITING

Do you think gambling is good or bad? Write six sentences or a short paragraph. Give your reasons. If you write a paragraph, be sure to indent the first sentence.

EXAMPLE: _____ I think gambling is bad. It is a waste of money. _____

_____

_____

THE WHITE HOUSE

PREREADING

What do you know about the White House? Circle T or F.

		True	False
1.	The president lives in the White House.	T	F
2.	In the beginning, the White House was gray.	T	F
3.	George Washington designed the White House.	T	F
4.	George Washington was the first president to live in the White House.	T	F
5.	The British burned the White House in 1814.	T	F
6.	Tourists cannot go inside the White House.	T	F

In Washington, D.C., 1600 Pennsylvania Avenue is a very special address. It is the address of the White House, the home of the president of the United States.

Originally the White House was gray and was called the Presidential Palace. It was built from 1792 to 1800. At this time, the city of Washington itself was being built. It was to be the nation's new capital city. George Washington, the first president, and Pierre-Charles L'Enfant, a French engineer, chose the place for the new city. L'Enfant then planned the city. The president's home was an important part of the plan.

A contest was held to pick a design for the president's home. An architect named James Hoban won. He designed a large three-story house of gray stone.

President Washington never lived in the Presidential Palace. The first people to live there were John Adams, the second president of the United States, and his wife, Abigail. Abigail Adams did not really like her new house. In her letters, she often complained about the cold. Fifty fireplaces were not enough to keep the house warm!

In 1812 the United States and Britain went to war. In 1814 the British invaded Washington. They burned many buildings, including the Presidential Palace.

After the war Hoban, the original architect, partially rebuilt the president's home. To cover the marks of the fire, the building was painted white. Before long it became known as the White House.

The White House is one of the most popular tourist attractions in the United States. Every year more than 1.5 million visitors go through the five rooms that are open to the public.

VOCABULARY

Complete the sentences. Circle the letter of the correct answer.

1. _____ the White House was gray. Now it is white.
   a. Partially   **b.** Originally

2. There was a contest to _____ the best design for the home of the president.
   a. plan   **b.** pick

3. James Hoban was the _____ who designed the plans for the president's home.
   a. engineer   **b.** architect

4. Abigail Adams _____ about how cold her new home was. She wrote about this problem in her letters.
   a. complained   **b.** invaded

5. After the war, not all of the White House needed to be rebuilt, but it did need to be _____ rebuilt.
   a. originally   **b.** partially

6. Most of the rooms in the White House are private, but there are five rooms that anyone can visit. These rooms are open to the _____ .

    a. public   **b.** popular

COMPREHENSION

A. Looking for Main Ideas

Write complete answers to these questions.

1. Who lives in the White House?

_____

2. Why was the White House built in Washington?

_____

3. Why did the original home of the president need to be rebuilt?

_____

B. Looking for Details

Circle the letter of the best answer.

1. The _____ is 1600 Pennsylvania Avenue.
    a. address of Washington, D.C.
    b. address of the White House
    c. original name of the White House

2. The Presidential Palace was _____ .
    a. painted white
    b. made of white stone
    c. made of gray stone

3. The president's home and the city of Washington were built _____ .
    a. by the British
    b. at the same time
    c. by the French

4. The first president to live in the Presidential Palace was _____ .
    a. George Washington
    b. Abigail Adams
    c. John Adams

5. The Presidential Palace was burned down by _____ .
    a. Abigail Adams
    b. James Hoban
    c. the British

6. The new presidential home was painted white to _____ .
    a. attract tourists
    b. cover the marks of the fire
    c. please Abigail Adams

GRAMMAR

Replace the underlined pronouns in the sentences with the correct nouns or phrases.

The British	Abigail Adams	The White House
James Hoban	White paint	George Washington
The United States	Britain	Pierre-Charles L'Enfant

1. <u>It</u> is the home of the president of the United States.

2. <u>They</u> burned the Presidential Palace.

3. <u>They</u> chose the place for the new city of Washington.

4. <u>She</u> did not like her new house.

5. <u>He</u> entered a contest to design the Presidential Palace.

6. <u>It</u> covered the marks of the fire.

7. <u>He</u> never lived in the Presidential Palace.

8. <u>They</u> went to war in 1812.

DISCUSSION

Discuss the answers to these questions with your classmates.

1. What other famous U.S. buildings can you name?

2. If you had to choose a new capital for the United States, where would you put it?

3. Where does the leader of your country live?

WRITING

Write six sentences or a short paragraph about the building where the leader of your country lives or about your country's capital city. If you write a paragraph, be sure to indent the first sentence.

EXAMPLE: My country's capital city is Tokyo. It has a very big
population.

_____

_____

HOLLYWOOD

Unit
12

PREREADING

Name some famous Hollywood movie stars, dead or alive.

Men   **Women**

To many people, the word *Hollywood* has two meanings. Hollywood is an area in Los Angeles. Hollywood is also the American movie industry.

Hollywood was just farmland at the beginning of this century. Early American movies were made in other places; for example, in New York and Chicago.

In 1917 a director was making a movie in Chicago. Because of cold weather, he couldn't finish the movie. He took a trip to southern California, and there he found just the weather and scenery he needed to finish his movie. The director realized that southern California was the perfect place for making movies. The next year his company built a movie studio in Hollywood. Other companies followed. Before long nearly all important American movie studios were in Hollywood.

The next thirty years were Hollywood's greatest years. Thousands of movies were made, most by a few large and powerful studios. Directors, actors, and writers worked for these studios. They made some movies that today are considered great art.

Hollywood, the area in Los Angeles, also reached its high point in these years. Many famous and glamorous movie stars, like Bette Davis and Clark Gable, lived in Hollywood.

Today, Hollywood is not what it was. More movies are made outside of Hollywood. Many studios have moved. The movie stars have also moved to areas like Beverly Hills and Malibu.

But visitors to Hollywood today can go to the famous Chinese Theater and see the footprints and autographs of movie stars. They can go down the Walk of Fame, on Hollywood Boulevard, and see the golden stars in the sidewalk.

VOCABULARY

Complete the sentences with one of the following words.

glamorous	Nearly	autograph	industry
powerful	scenery	century	

1. Directors, actors, and writers all work in the movie business

   or _____ .

2. One hundred years is a _____ .

3. The mountains, ocean, and trees all make California's _____ beautiful.

4. _____ all the people came to the party. Thirty-six were invited and thirty-two came.

5. The United States is a very _____ country. It has a lot of influence over other countries.

6. The actress looked very _____ in her beautiful dress and diamond jewelry.

7. When a famous person signs his or her name, it is called an _____ .

COMPREHENSION

A. Looking for Main Ideas

Circle the letter of the best answer.

1. Hollywood today means two things: _____ .
   a. the movie industry and farmland
   b. farmland and perfect scenery
   c. an area in Los Angeles and the movie industry

2. The great years of Hollywood were _____ .
   a. 1917 and the next year
   b. from 1918 to 1948
   c. after 1948

3. Today, most movies are made _____ .
   a. in Beverly Hills
   b. in Hollywood
   c. outside Hollywood

B. Looking for Details

Circle T if the sentence is true. Circle F if the sentence is false.

		True	False
1.	Some early American movies were made in Chicago and New York.	T	F
2.	In 1917 a director went to California because he had a cold.	T	F
3.	The first movie studio was built in Hollywood in 1918.	T	F
4.	A thousand movies were made in thirty years.	T	F
5.	Some movies are considered great art.	T	F
6.	Today many studios have moved to Beverly Hills and Malibu.	T	F

GRAMMAR

Complete the sentences with the prepositions below.

at	in	to	for	from

EXAMPLE: Famous movie stars like Bette Davis lived ___in___ Hollywood.

1. Hollywood means two things _____ many people.

2. Hollywood is an area _____ Los Angeles.

3. Hollywood was farmland _____ the beginning of this century.

4. Some early American movies were made _____ Chicago and New York.

5. The director's company built a studio _____ Hollywood _____ 1918.

6. Directors and actors worked _____ large studios.

7. Many actors have moved _____ Hollywood _____ Malibu.

8. Visitors can go _____ the Chinese Theater.

DISCUSSION

Discuss the answers to these questions with your classmates.

1. Why do people still go to the movies when they can rent a video or watch a movie on TV?

2. What is a good movie to see this year?

3. Would you like to be a famous movie star? Why or why not?

WRITING

Write a short paragraph about a movie you watched recently. Be sure to indent the first sentence.

EXAMPLE: _I went to the movies recently. I saw the movie Men in Black. . . ._

_____

_____

MALLS

Unit 13

PREREADING

Check the things you think people can do in a shopping mall.

_____ see a movie	_____ go to the dentist
_____ go to church	_____ see a doctor
_____ rent a car	_____ go dancing
_____ buy groceries	_____ take classes

Malls are popular places for Americans to go. Some people spend so much time at malls that they are called "mall rats." Mall rats "shop until they drop" in the hundreds of stores under one roof.

People like malls for many reasons. They feel safe because malls have police stations or private security guards. Parking is usually free, and the weather inside is always fine. The newest malls have beautiful rest areas with waterfalls and palm trees.

The largest mall in the United States is the Mall of America in Minnesota. It covers 4.2 million square feet. It has 350 stores, eight nightclubs, and a seven-acre amusement park! There are parking spaces for 12,750 cars. About 750,000 people shop there every week.

The first indoor mall in the United States was built in 1965 in Edina, Minnesota. People loved doing all their shopping in one place. Many more malls were built all over the country. Now, malls are like town centers where people come to do many things. They shop, of course. They also eat in food courts that have food from all over the world. They see movies at multiplex theaters. Some people even get their daily exercise by doing the new sport of "mall walking." Others go to malls to meet friends.

In some malls, people can see a doctor or a dentist and even attend church. In other words, people can do just about everything in malls. The latest trend is condo-malls. Now residents can actually live in their favorite shopping center. For a mall rat, this is a dream come true.

VOCABULARY

Complete the sentences. Circle the letter of the correct answer.

1. A place where there are big machines to ride on and games for people to play is _____ .

   a. a town center   **b.** an amusement park   **c.** a rest area

2. _____ are places where you can find tables and chairs and many open restaurants.

   a. Food courts   **b.** Theaters   **c.** Nightclubs

3. Water falling straight down over large stones often creates the sound and beauty of _____ .

   a. waterfalls   **b.** palm trees   **c.** fish ponds

4. People who live in a certain place are its _____ .

   a. shoppers   **b.** guards   **c.** residents

5. A _____ has several theaters all in one building or part of a building.

   a. mall   **b.** multiplex   **c.** condo

6. The latest style or way of doing things is _____ .

   a. an exercise   **b.** an area   **c.** a trend

7. Places that have stores and living places in the same building are called _____ .

   a. condo-malls   **b.** shopping centers   **c.** apartments

8. _____ is 4,840 square yards or 4,047 square meters. You need many in order to have enough space to build a mall.

    a. An area   **b.** An acre   **c.** A place

COMPREHENSION

A. Looking for Main Ideas

Circle the letter of the best answer.

1. People like malls because they _____ .
     a. are safe, beautiful, and have parking spaces
     b. are places where dreams can come true
     c. have areas where drivers can rest

2. The largest mall in America _____ .
     a. is built mostly for children
     b. sells thousands of cars to shoppers
     c. has both shopping and entertainment

3. Malls became popular because people like to _____ .
     a. shop and do things all in one place
     b. live in the same place where they shop
     c. see more than one movie at a time

B. Looking for Details

One word in each sentence is not correct. Cross out the word and write the correct answer above it.

1. Mall rats spend a lot of time at zoos.

2. Parking is usually expensive at malls.

3. The smallest mall in the United States is in Minnesota.

4. The first indoor mall in the United States was built in 1948 in Edina, Minnesota.

5. Food courts have gifts from all over the world.

6. People get their friends by "mall walking."

GRAMMAR

Complete the sentences with the prepositions below.

for	in	with	from	to

EXAMPLE: Malls are popular places ____for____ Americans to go.

1. Some malls have rest areas _____ waterfalls and palm trees.

2. There is an amusement park _____ the Mall of America.

3. The Mall of America has parking spaces _____ 12,750 cars.

4. Some malls have food _____ all over the world.

5. Some people go _____ malls to meet friends.

6. _____ some malls, people can see a doctor or a dentist.

DISCUSSION

Discuss the answers to these questions with your classmates.

1. Why do you think people like to shop in malls?

2. Would you like to live in a condo-mall? Why or why not?

3. What is there about malls that you like? What is there about malls that you don't like?

WRITING

Write six sentences or a short paragraph about the way people shop in your country. If you write a paragraph, be sure to indent the first sentence.

EXAMPLE: _In my country we do not have malls. Most towns have a downtown area with nice stores._

_____

_____

HARRIET BEECHER STOWE

Unit 14

PREREADING

Give the titles of some world-famous novels.

Sometimes a book can help change history. One book that certainly did was *Uncle Tom's Cabin,* written by Harriet Beecher Stowe. It was a book that spoke out against slavery.

At the time Harriet Beecher Stowe wrote her novel, there were over 3.5 million slaves in the United States. Slaves were usually in the cotton-growing states of the South. The Northern states had abolished, or gotten rid of, slavery. Yet most Northerners were not strongly against slavery. They were willing to let slavery continue in the South.

Stowe was determined to make people understand that slavery was evil. Each night after putting her six children to bed, she worked on her novel. She told the story of characters like Tom, a courageous old slave, Simon Legree, a cruel man who buys Tom, and Eliza, who makes a dangerous escape to freedom.

Uncle Tom's Cabin was published in 1852. Over 300,000 copies were sold in a year.

People reacted strongly to the novel. In the North, many people were finally convinced that slavery must be ended. In the South, many people were very angry.

Disagreements between the North and the South grew. By 1861 the two sections of the country were at war. The Civil War, which lasted until 1865, finally brought an end to slavery.

Of course, the Civil War had many different causes. Yet *Uncle Tom's Cabin* surely played a part. Stowe met President Lincoln in 1862. As Lincoln took her hand, he said, "So you're the little woman who started the big war."

VOCABULARY

Replace the underlined words in the sentences with the words below.

published	novel	Slaves
spoke out	causes	escape

1. Harriet Beecher Stowe's book <u>protested</u> against slavery.

2. Harriet Beecher Stowe wrote a <u>book that tells a story</u>.

3. <u>People who were not free</u> worked in the Southern cotton fields.

4. Some slaves tried to <u>get away</u>.

5. *Uncle Tom's Cabin* was <u>made into a book available to the public</u> in 1852.

6. The American Civil War had many <u>reasons for happening</u>.

COMPREHENSION

A. Looking for Main Ideas

Circle the letter of the best answer.

1. *Uncle Tom's Cabin* was a _____ .
   a. book about Harriet Beecher Stowe
   b. book that helped change history
   c. history book

2. Harriet Beecher Stowe wanted _____ .
   a. people to understand that slavery was evil
   b. people to have slaves
   c. slavery to continue in the South

3. *Uncle Tom's Cabin* _____ .
   a. played a part in starting the American Civil War
   b. was written by Abraham Lincoln
   c. told the story of the American Civil War

B. Looking for Details

Circle the letter of the best answer.

1. When Harriet Beecher Stowe wrote her book, there were _____ .
   a. slaves only in the North
   b. 3.5 million slaves in the United States

2. Harriet Beecher Stowe wrote her book _____ .
   a. after she put her six children to bed
   b. with stories from her six children

3. Before *Uncle Tom's Cabin*, most Northerners _____ .
   a. were slaves in the South
   b. were willing to let slavery continue in the South

4. Harriet Beecher Stowe's book about slavery sold _____ .
   a. 3.5 million copies in one year
   b. over 300,000 copies in one year

5. While many Northerners agreed with Harriet Beecher Stowe, _____ .
   a. many Southerners wanted war
   b. many Southerners were angry

GRAMMAR

Combine the two sentences into one using *and* or *but*.

EXAMPLE: Stowe told the story of Tom, a courageous old slave.
Stowe told the story of Simon Legree, a cruel man who buys Tom.

Stowe told the story of Tom, a courageous old

slave, and Simon Legree, a cruel man who buys

Tom.

1. *Uncle Tom's Cabin* was written by Harriet Beecher Stowe. *Uncle Tom's Cabin* was published in 1852.

2. Slavery had been abolished in the North. Most Northerners were willing to let slavery continue in the South.

3. Harriet Beecher Stowe had six children. Harriet Beecher Stowe wrote every night after she put them to bed.

4. People in the North agreed with *Uncle Tom's Cabin*. People in the South were angry.

5. Disagreements between the North and the South grew. By 1861 there was war.

6. The Civil War lasted until 1865. The Civil War brought an end to slavery.

DISCUSSION

Discuss the answers to these questions with your classmates.

1. Do you know any other books that have gotten strong reactions from people? What books have you read that made you react strongly?

2. How many famous black Americans can you name?

WRITING

Write six sentences or a short paragraph about a book or article you read or heard about that made you react strongly. If you write a paragraph, be sure to indent the first sentence.

EXAMPLE: I read an article about a man who murdered another man.
He went to prison for five years, and now he is free.

John F. Kennedy

PREREADING

What do you know about President John F. Kennedy? Circle T or F.

		True	False
1.	John Kennedy came from a small family.	T	F
2.	The Kennedys were very rich.	T	F
3.	John Kennedy was very athletic and strong as a child.	T	F
4.	John Kennedy was popular because of his new ideas.	T	F
5.	John Kennedy did not fight in World War II.	T	F
6.	John Kennedy was shot.	T	F

In November 1960, John Fitzgerald Kennedy became the youngest president of the United States. People liked him because he had new ideas. John Kennedy gave Americans hope for the future.

Kennedy was born on May 29, 1917. He was the second of nine children. His family was one of the most wealthy and powerful in America. His father, Joseph, was so rich that he gave each of his children one million dollars when they reached the age of twenty-one. Kennedy's mother, Rose, lived to the age of 104. Her religious faith and strength of character helped the family through its tragedies and triumphs.

As a child, Kennedy was sickly. He admired his brother, Joe, who was athletic and intelligent. Their father wanted Joe to be president one day. But Joe was killed during World War II. John was almost killed too.

A Japanese warship hit his boat, but he survived the crash. He won a medal for saving his men.

After the war, John Kennedy began a career in politics. When he became president, he gave a famous speech. He promised to work for freedom around the world. He asked people to give something of themselves. "Ask not what your country can do for you," he said. "Ask what you can do for your country."

Kennedy was very popular during his early presidency. People liked him and his wife, Jacqueline. She was young, beautiful, and elegant. People loved to see photos of the Kennedys with their two children, John and Caroline. They were the first children in the White House in fifty years.

Kennedy began the space program that put a man on the moon in 1969. He also started the Peace Corps. Thousands of young Americans volunteered to work where they were needed in countries around the world.

On November 22, 1963, John F. Kennedy was assassinated in Dallas, Texas. The world was filled with shock and sorrow.

VOCABULARY

Complete the definitions. Circle the letter of the correct answer.

1. When things happen that make people sad, they are called _____ .
   a. ideas   **b.** tragedies   **c.** powers

2. When people or things have beauty and style, they are _____ .
   a. elegant   **b.** famous   **c.** athletic

3. When you have a lot of money, you are _____ .
   a. intelligent   **b.** wealthy   **c.** brave

4. When you are sad, you feel _____ .
   a. surprise   **b.** strength   **c.** sorrow

5. When a person wins a battle or has success, it is called a _____ .
   a. promise   **b.** dream   **c.** triumph

6. When people are killed for political reasons, they are _____ .
   a. assassinated   **b.** elected   **c.** volunteered

7. When you believe strongly in something, you have _____ .

    a. faith   **b.** hope   **c.** generosity

8. When people have a good opinion of someone, that person is _____ .

    a. helped   **b.** admired   **c.** rewarded

COMPREHENSION

A. Looking for Main Ideas

Circle the letter of the best answer.

1. Americans voted for John F. Kennedy because _____ .

    a. he came from a wealthy family

    b. he was still a young man

    c. they thought his ideas were good for the country

2. Kennedy wanted _____ .

    a. more people to have careers in politics

    b. people all over the world to be free

    c. government to do more for the American people

3. During his presidency, Kennedy _____ .

    a. began some important programs

    b. saved the lives of many people

    c. became wealthy and powerful

B. Looking for Details

Number the sentences 1 through 7 to show the correct order.

_____ Kennedy saved the lives of many men.

_____ Kennedy was assassinated in Dallas, Texas.

_____ Kennedy became president.

_____ John F. Kennedy was born into one of the most wealthy and powerful families in America.

_____ Kennedy began the space program that one day put a man on the moon.

_____ Kennedy was almost killed when a Japanese warship hit his boat.

_____ Kennedy won a medal for his bravery.

GRAMMAR

Complete the sentences using the past tense form of the verbs in parentheses.

EXAMPLE: In 1960, John Kennedy ___*became*___ the youngest
(become)
president in U.S. history.

1. John Kennedy _____ his older brother, Joe.
(admire)

2. When a Japanese warship hit his boat, Kennedy _____ the crash.
(survive)

3. Kennedy _____ a medal for his bravery during World War II.
(win)

4. After the war, Kennedy _____ a career in politics.
(begin)

5. After his election as president, Kennedy _____ a famous speech.
(give)

6. Kennedy _____ the Peace Corps.
(start)

DISCUSSION

Discuss the answers to these questions with your classmates.

1. Imagine you are president right now. What kinds of things would you do for the country?

2. John F. Kennedy wanted people to give something of themselves to their country. What kinds of things can people do to make their country a better place to live?

3. Who do you think makes a better leader, an older person with experience or a younger person with new ideas. Why?

WRITING

Write six sentences or a short paragraph. Give reasons why you would or wouldn't like to have a career in politics. If you write a paragraph, be sure to indent the first sentence.

EXAMPLE: _I would not like to have a career in politics. First, it is too much responsibility._

_____

_____

BILL GATES

PREREADING

Look at the list of words below. Underline the words that are associated with computers. Do you know the meaning of these words? How many other words about computers can you add to the list?

mouse	disk
book	keyboard
pencil	memory
software	monitor
paper clip	audiocassette

Personal computers, or PCs, are an important part of our everyday lives. Many people cannot imagine life without them. One of the most important people in making these machines work is Bill Gates.

Bill Gates was born in 1955 in Washington State. He grew up in a rich family. His parents sent him to private school. There he met his business partner, Paul Allen. When they were in the eighth grade, they were writing programs for business computers and making money.

In 1973, Gates was accepted at Harvard University. His parents were happy. They thought he would get over his obsession with computers and become a lawyer like his father. Two years later, Gates dropped out of Harvard to work on a computer program with his friend Allen. They worked eighteen hours a day in a dormitory room at

Harvard. They were writing the program that would run one of the first personal computers. In 1975, they created a company called Microsoft to sell their product.

Allen became ill with cancer and left Microsoft in 1983. He recovered a few years later and started his own company. Meanwhile, Microsoft became a giant company. By 1990, at the age of thirty-four, Gates was the youngest billionaire in the history of the United States. He was the "King of Software." He achieved his success with a lot of hard work. For more than ten years, he worked sixteen-hour days, seven days a week. He had a dream and the will to succeed. By 1997, he was the richest man in the United States.

VOCABULARY

Replace the underlined words in the sentences with the words below.

obsession with	giant	dropped out of	software
dormitory	will	get over	achieved

1. Bill Gates <u>earned</u> his success by working very hard.

2. Bill Gate's parents wanted him to <u>no longer have</u> his obsession with computers.

3. In a few years, Microsoft became a <u>very large</u> company.

4. Bill Gates and Paul Allen worked eighteen hours a day in their <u>building where students live</u> at Harvard.

5. When Bill Gates went to college, his parents thought he would get over his <u>uncontrollable interest in</u> computers.

6. Bill Gates has a <u>strong wish</u> to succeed.

7. Paul Allen started his own company to sell <u>computer programs</u>.

8. After two years, Bill Gates <u>stopped taking classes at</u> Harvard.

COMPREHENSION

A. Looking for Main Ideas

Write the questions to these answers.

1. _____ ?

   Bill Gates met his business partner in school.

2. _____ ?

   Bill Gates and Paul Allen created Microsoft because they wanted to sell their program for personal computers.

3. _____ ?

   Bill Gates worked sixteen-hour days, seven days a week for more than ten years.

B. Looking for Details

Circle the letter of the best answer.

1. Bill Gates was born in _____ .
   a. New York
   b. Washington
   c. California

2. In 1973, Bill Gates was accepted at _____ .
   a. Microsoft
   b. Harvard
   c. computer school

3. Bill Gates's parents wanted him to become a _____ .
   a. computer programmer
   b. teacher
   c. lawyer

4. When Gates and Allen were in the eighth grade, they were writing programs for _____ .
   a. business computers
   b. personal computers
   c. private schools

5. Paul Allen left Microsoft because _____ .
   a. he wanted to start his own company
   b. he was ill
   c. he became rich

6. In 1990, Bill Gates became the youngest _____ in U.S. history.
   a. company president
   b. college student
   c. billionaire

GRAMMAR

Combine the two sentences into one using _and_ or _but_.

EXAMPLE: Bill Gates grew up in a rich family. Bill Gates went to a
private school.

Bill Gates grew up in a rich family and went to a private

school.

1. Many people cannot imagine life without PCs. PCs are actually a recent invention.

2. In the eighth grade, Paul Allen and Bill Gates were writing programs for business computers. In the eighth grade, Paul Allen and Bill Gates were making money.

3. Gates's parents wanted their son to become a lawyer. He dropped out of Harvard two years later.

4. Paul Allen recovered from cancer. Paul Allen started his own company.

5. At the age of thirty-four, Bill Gates was a billionaire. At the age of thirty-four, Bill Gates was the "King of Software."

6. Bill Gates had a dream. Bill Gates had the will to succeed.

DISCUSSION

Discuss the answers to these questions with your classmates.

1. What are some ways of getting rich in your country?

2. In your country, which is more highly regarded, inherited wealth or wealth gained from business? Why?

3. The world has become very dependent on computers. Do you think this is a good thing? Why or why not?

WRITING

Write a short paragraph about a person who is or was successful. Tell the story of how the person became successful. Be sure to indent the first sentence.

EXAMPLE: My uncle is a successful businessperson. He owns a
factory in my country.

NOAH WEBSTER

Unit 17

PREREADING

British English and American English spell some words differently. Which of these words belong to an American English dictionary? Which belong to a British English dictionary? Can you think of any more?

color/colour	grey/gray	program/programme
honour/honor	surprise/surprize	center/centre
advertise/advertize	cheque/check	

American English	**British English**
color	colour

As a young adult, Noah Webster was a teacher. At this time, the colonies were fighting for independence from Britain. Yet the books that American children used in school all came from Britain. The books were all about British people and British places. Webster wanted books that would mean more to American children. So he wrote three books that used American examples—a grammar book, a spelling book, and a reader. These books were very popular, and millions of them were sold.

Webster was interested in changing the spellings of words. He wanted words to be spelled the way they were pronounced. For example, he thought the word *head* should be spelled "hed," and the word *laugh* should be spelled "laf." People liked Webster's suggestions.

Unfortunately, though, few words were changed. One group of words that were changed were words in which an unpronounced *u* followed an *o.* That is why Americans write *color* and *labor,* and the British write *colour* and *labour.*

With the money he made from his books, Webster was able to start on his great work. This work took more than twenty years to write. It was the first American English dictionary, published in 1828. Webster's dictionary had over 70,000 words and gave the meaning and origin of each. To this day, Webster's work is the example that most dictionaries of American English follow.

VOCABULARY

Complete the definitions. Circle the letter of the correct answer.

1. A person that is not a child is _____ .
   a. an adult   **b.** a teacher   **c.** British

2. An idea you share with other people is a _____ .
   a. dictionary   **b.** suggestion   **c.** sentence

3. Sounds that are not spoken are _____ .
   a. definitions   **b.** unpronounced   **c.** spelled

4. The beginning or the start of something is its _____ .
   a. meaning   **b.** spelling   **c.** origin

5. When books are printed they are _____ .
   a. pronounced   **b.** published   **c.** changed

COMPREHENSION

A. Looking for Main Ideas

Write complete answers to these questions.

1. What three books did Noah Webster write for school children?

   _____

2. Why did Webster want to change the spellings of words?

   _____

3. What was Webster's most famous work?

_____

B. Looking for Details

Circle T if the sentence is true. Circle F if the sentence is false.

		True	False
1. American children used to use British schoolbooks.		T	F
2. Webster's books sold one million copies.		T	F
3. Webster wanted to change the spelling of words.		T	F
4. The American spelling of the word _color_ is different from the British spelling.		T	F
5. Webster's dictionary took exactly twenty years to write.		T	F
6. Webster's dictionary was the first American English dictionary.		T	F
7. Webster's dictionary had 7,000 words.		T	F
8. Webster's dictionary gave both the meaning and the origin of words.		T	F

GRAMMAR

Replace the underlined pronouns in the sentences with the correct nouns or phrases.

The books	Webster's dictionary	his great work
few words	American children	The British
the money	spellings	Noah Webster

1. He was a teacher.

2. They used British books.

3. They were all about British people and places.

4. Webster tried to change them.

5. Unfortunately, they were changed.

6. They write _colour_.

7. With it, Webster was able to start on it.

8. It is the example for most dictionaries.

DISCUSSION

Discuss the answers to these questions with your classmates.

1. Why is a dictionary useful?

2. Do you think spelling words in American English is difficult? Why or why not?

3. Is spelling difficult in your language? Is it more or less difficult than spelling in English?

WRITING

Write six sentences or a short paragraph. What do you think is easy to learn about the English language? What do you think is difficult? If you write a paragraph, be sure to indent the first sentence.

EXAMPLE: I think nouns are easy to learn in English because they have no masculine or feminine form as in my language. Spelling is very difficult, however.

HENRY FORD

Unit 18

Name American and other well-known car companies around the world.

American Car Companies	**Other Car Companies**

Henry Ford was born in 1863 in the state of Michigan. He grew up on a farm, but he did not want to become a farmer. He left school when he was sixteen. He wanted to make cars so he went to work as a mechanic.

In 1896 Ford built his first car. This car was very different from the cars of today. For example, its wheels were bicycle wheels.

In 1902 Ford built a car that won an important race. This car was the fastest car that had ever been built. It went seventy miles per hour. By then Ford had enough money to start the Ford Motor Company.

At this time, cars cost a lot of money. Only very rich people bought cars. Ford had a dream. He wanted to build a car that many people could afford. Ford was sure that, if people could afford cars, they would buy them. He said, "Everybody wants to be somewhere he isn't."

Ford's plan was to make all his cars the same. Cars that are all the same take less time and less money to make. Then Ford could charge less money for these cars. In 1908 Ford produced his famous Model T Ford. The Model T sold for $850. This was much cheaper than other cars but still more than most people could pay.

One day Ford visited a meat-packing factory. There he saw animal carcasses being moved from one worker to another. Each worker had a particular job to do when a carcass reached him. Ford realized that he could use this assembly line method to build cars.

It took less than two hours to build a car on the assembly line. Before, it took fourteen hours. Ford was able to drop the price of the Model T to $265.

Ford's dream had come true. The Model T was now a car that many people could afford. By 1927, when Ford stopped making the Model T, over 15 million of these cars had been sold.

VOCABULARY

Which sentences have the same meaning as the sentences from the reading? Circle the letter of the correct answer.

1. Ford went to work as a mechanic.
   a. Ford fixed cars.
   b. Ford sold cars.

2. He wanted to build a car that many people could afford.
   a. He wanted to build a car many people would have enough money to buy.
   b. He wanted to build a car people would be able to sell easily.

3. He could charge less money for a car.
   a. He could ask people to use a credit card.
   b. He could ask people to pay less money.

4. Ford saw animal carcasses at the factory.
   a. Ford saw animals in boxes at the factory.
   b. Ford saw the bodies of dead animals at the factory.

5. Ford realized that he could use this assembly line method to build cars.
   a. Ford understood that the assembly line was a good way to build cars.
   b. Ford invented the assembly line equipment to build cars.

COMPREHENSION

A. Looking for Main Ideas

Circle the letter of the best answer.

1. Henry Ford built _____ .
   a. the first car
   b. the first bicycle
   c. a car with bicycle wheels

2. Henry Ford's dream was _____ .
   a. to build an assembly line
   b. to build a car most people could afford
   c. to build a car that would win a race

3. Ford first saw an assembly line _____ .
   a. at a meat-packing factory
   b. on a farm
   c. at the Ford Motor Company

B. Looking for Details

Circle T if the sentence is true. Circle F if the sentence is false.

	True	False
1. Henry Ford left school when he was sixteen.	T	F
2. Henry Ford made bicycle wheels on the farm.	T	F
3. Ford built a car that went seventy miles per hour.	T	F
4. Only very poor people bought cars.	T	F
5. Ford said, "Everybody wants to be what he isn't."	T	F
6. The 1908 Model T cost more than most people could pay.	T	F
7. Before the assembly line, it took fourteen hours to build two cars.	T	F
8. Ford dropped the price of the Model T by $585.	T	F

GRAMMAR

Complete the sentences using the past tense form of the verbs in parentheses.

EXAMPLE: Henry Ford's dream _____*came*_____ true.
                                    (come)

1. Ford _____ on a farm.
        (grow up)

2. When he was sixteen, he _____ school.
                              (leave)

3. He _____ to work as a mechanic.
        (go)

4. He _____ his first car in 1896.
        (build)

5. Ford's 1902 car _____ an important race.
                        (win)

6. In those days, cars _____ a lot of money.
                          (cost)

7. Only very rich people _____ cars.
                            (buy)

8. The first Model T _____ for $850.
                        (sell)

DISCUSSION

Discuss the answers to these questions with your classmates.

1. Which car do you think is most popular in the United States?

2. What do you think the car of the future will look like?

3. There are more and more cars on the roads. What can be done to solve our traffic problems?

WRITING

Write six sentences or a short paragraph. What is the perfect car for you? What can it do? What does it look like? If you write a paragraph, be sure to indent the first sentence.

EXAMPLE: The perfect car for me looks like a Ferrari. It is red.

_____

_____

THE HOT DOG

Unit 19

PREREADING

Name some snack foods people eat in your country.

In its home country of Germany, the hot dog was called the *frankfurter.* It was named after Frankfurt, a German city.

Frankfurters were first sold in the United States in the 1860s. Americans called frankfurters "dachshund sausages." A dachshund is a dog from Germany with a very long body and short legs. "Dachshund sausage" seemed like a good name for the frankfurter.

Dachshund sausages first became popular in New York, especially at baseball games. At games they were sold by men who kept them warm in hot-water tanks. As the men walked up and down the rows of people, they yelled, "Get your dachshund sausages! Get your hot dachshund sausages!" People got the sausages on a special bread called buns.

One day in 1906, a newspaper cartoonist named Tad Dorgan went to a baseball game. When he saw the men with the dachshund sausages, he got an idea for a cartoon. The next day at the newspaper office, he drew a bun with a dachshund inside—not a dachshund sausage, but a dachshund. Dorgan didn't know how to spell *dachshund.* Under the cartoon, he wrote "Get your hot dogs!"

The cartoon was a sensation and so was the new name. If you go to a baseball game today, you can still see sellers walking around with hot-water tanks. As they walk up and down the rows, they yell, "Get your hot dogs here! Get your hot dogs!"

VOCABULARY

Complete the definitions. Circle the letter of the correct answer.

1. The special bread used for a hot dog is a ———— .
   a. sausage   **b.** bun   **c.** dachshund

2. Another word for *to shout* is to ———— .
   a. name   **b.** draw   **c.** yell

3. A line of objects or people is a ———— .
   a. row   **b.** game   **c.** cartoon

4. When something is a cause of excitement, it is ———— .
   a. an idea   **b.** a sensation   **c.** a hot dog

5. Large containers for water or other liquids, sometimes made of metal, are called ———— .
   a. tanks   **b.** sellers   **c.** cartoonists

6. A funny drawing is a ———— .
   a. cartoonist   **b.** frankfurter   **c.** cartoon

COMPREHENSION

A. Looking for Main Ideas

Write the questions for these answers.

1. What _____?
   Americans called frankfurters "dachshund sausages."

2. Where in the United States _____?
   Dachshund sausages were first sold at baseball games.

3. Who _____?
   Tad Dorgan was a newspaper cartoonist.

B. Looking for Details

Circle T if the sentence is true. Circle F if the sentence is false.

		True	False
1.	Frankfurters were first sold in the United States in the 1960s.	T	F
2.	A dachshund is a dog with a long body and short legs.	T	F
3.	At baseball games today you cannot see sellers walking around with hot-water tanks.	T	F
4.	Tad Dorgan got an idea for a cartoon in his office.	T	F
5.	Tad Dorgan drew a bun with a sausage inside.	T	F
6.	The words under Tad Dorgan's cartoon were "Get your hot dogs!"	T	F

GRAMMAR

Complete the sentences using the past tense form of the verbs in parentheses.

EXAMPLE: Americans ___called___ frankfurters "dachshund sausages."
                              (call)

1. Dachshund sausages first _____ popular in New York.
                                  (become)

2. The sellers _____ the sausages warm in hot-water tanks.
                   (keep)

3. People _____ the sausages on buns.
              (get)

4. One day Tad Dorgan _____ to a baseball game.
(go)

5. He _____ the men with the dachshund sausages.
(see)

6. He _____ "Get your hot dogs!" under his cartoon.
(write)

DISCUSSION

Discuss the answers to these questions with your classmates.

1. Besides hot dogs, what are other popular foods in the United States? What are some popular foods in your country?

2. Are hot dogs healthy for you? Why or why not?

3. What are some healthy foods? What are some foods that are not so healthy?

WRITING

Write six sentences or a short paragraph about a snack food or sandwich you like. How do you make it? When do you eat it? If you write a paragraph, be sure to indent the first sentence.

EXAMPLE: _My favorite snack food is a pita bread sandwich. I take a_
small pita bread. . . .

_____

_____

The Cranberry

Unit 20

PREREADING

What do you know about cranberries? Circle T or F.

	True	False
1. Cranberries are sweet.	T	F
2. Cranberries grow everywhere in the United States.	T	F
3. Cranberries get ripe in cold weather.	T	F
4. Cranberries were used as medicine.	T	F
5. Americans eat cranberries at Thanksgiving dinner.	T	F

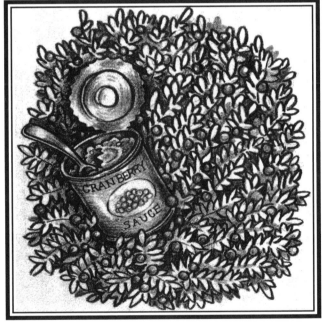

The cranberry is a North American fruit that grows on a bush. The cranberry is small, round, red, and very bitter. Native Americans used the berries for food and medicine. When settlers first came from England in the 1600s, they liked these berries, too. The settlers had never seen the berries before. They decided to call them "crane berries" because birds called cranes ate them.

The cranberry bush does not grow everywhere in the United States. In fact, it grows in only five states: Washington, Oregon, Wisconsin, Massachusetts, and New Jersey. These states have the special conditions that the cranberry bush needs.

Cranberries ripen when the weather starts to become cold. We see cranberries in the stores in the fall. Many people eat cranberries as part of the feast of Thanksgiving in November.

Sometimes cranberries are cooked and made into a sauce or a jelly. Cranberries taste less bitter after they are cooked.

Cranberry growers separate the best cranberries from all the rest. It's hard to recognize the best cranberries just by looking. So cranberry growers use a special method, which was developed by accident by a man named John Webb.

One day, as John Webb was taking a container of berries down some steps, he spilled the berries. While he was picking them up he noticed something interesting. The bad berries had stayed on the top steps, and the best berries had bounced down all the way to the bottom. Today, cranberry growers use a seven-step test to separate berries. The best cranberries are the ones that bounce down seven steps!

VOCABULARY

What is the meaning of the underlined words?

1. The cranberry grows on a bush.
   a. small fruit
   b. small tree

2. The Native Americans used the berries for food.
   a. fruit
   b. seeds

3. Cranberries are very bitter.
   a. not sweet
   b. good

4. Cranberries ripen when the weather starts to become cold.
   a. become ready to eat
   b. become bad

5. The best cranberries are the ones that bounce.
   a. jump up again
   b. do not jump

6. One day, John Webb <u>spilled</u> a container of berries.

    a. carried

    b. dropped

COMPREHENSION

A. Looking for Main Ideas

Write complete answers to these questions.

1. What is a cranberry?

_____

2. Where does the cranberry bush grow?

_____

3. Who developed the special method of separating the best cranberries from all the others?

_____

B. Looking for Details

One word in each sentence is *not* correct. Cross out the word and write the correct answer above it.

1. Cranberries taste more bitter after they are cooked.

2. John Webb noticed that the best berries had stayed on the top steps.

3. Cranberry growers use a seven-method test to separate berries.

4. The Native Americans decided to call the berries "crane berries."

5. Many people eat cranberries at Easter.

6. Cranberries can be cooled and made into a sauce or jelly.

7. Cranberries are in the stores in the summer.

8. It's easy to recognize the best cranberries just by looking.

GRAMMAR

Complete the sentences with the correct article. Use *a* or *the*. If no article is necessary, write *X*.

EXAMPLE: The cranberry grows on __*a*__ bush.

1. Native Americans used _____ berries for food and _____ medicine.

2. _____ cranberry bush does not grow everywhere in _____ United States of America.

3. Cranberries ripen when _____ weather starts to become cold.

4. We see _____ cranberries in _____ stores in _____ fall.

5. Many people eat cranberries as part of _____ feast of _____ Thanksgiving in _____ November.

6. Sometimes cranberries are made into _____ sauce or _____ jelly.

7. Cranberry growers separate _____ best cranberries from _____ rest.

8. Cranberry growers use _____ special method developed by _____ man named _____ John Webb.

DISCUSSION

Discuss the answers to these questions with your classmates.

1. What are some of the typical fruits that grow in your country?

2. What foods do you associate with other feasts or holidays you know?

3. What other fruits are commonly eaten as part of a main meal?

WRITING

Write six sentences or a short paragraph. Describe a special fruit or vegetable in your country. Say how it is used. If you write a paragraph, be sure to indent the first sentence.

EXAMPLE: The special fruit in my country, Armenia, is the pomegranate. Pomegranates grow on trees. They are like big apples.

_____

_____

Coca-Cola

PREREADING

What do you know about the history of Coca-Cola? Circle T or F.

	True	False
1. In the beginning, Coca-Cola was a medicine.	T	F
2. The brown syrup called Coca-Cola was a mix of coconuts and coffee.	T	F
3. People mixed Coca-Cola syrup with milk.	T	F
4. Before Coca-Cola was in bottles, people went to drugstores to drink it with soda water.	T	F
5. World War II made Coca-Cola popular outside the United States.	T	F
6. The Coca-Cola Company sent free bottles of Coca-Cola to soldiers fighting in Europe.	T	F

In 1886 John Pemberton, a druggist in Atlanta, Georgia, made a brown syrup by mixing coca leaves and cola nuts. Pemberton sold the syrup in his drugstore as a medicine to cure all kinds of problems. Pemberton called his all-purpose medicine "Coca-Cola."

When few people bought Coca-Cola, Pemberton sold the recipe to another druggist, Asa Candler. Candler decided to sell Coca-Cola as a soda-fountain drink instead of a medicine.

At the soda fountains in drugstores, the syrup was mixed with soda water to make the drink Coca-Cola. Candler advertised a lot and sold his syrup to many drugstores. Soon everyone was going to soda fountains and asking for Coca-Cola.

Candler saw no reason for putting Coca-Cola into bottles. But two businessmen thought this would be a good idea. They got permission from Candler, and before long they became millionaires.

As of 1903, coca leaves were no longer used in Coca-Cola. The exact ingredients used and their quantities are not known—the Coca-Cola Company keeps its recipe a secret.

World War I helped make Coca-Cola popular outside the United States. The Coca-Cola Company sent free bottles of the drink to U.S. soldiers fighting in Europe. Coca-Cola became very popular with the soldiers—so popular that the U.S. Army asked the company to start ten factories in Europe. After the war, these factories continued to make Coca-Cola. Today, there are Coca-Cola factories around the world.

VOCABULARY

Complete the sentences. Circle the letter of the correct answer.

1. A person who sells medicines is a _____ .
   a. druggist   **b.** millionaire   **c.** businessman

2. _____ is a sweet, heavy liquid that tastes good.
   a. Syrup   **b.** Cola   **c.** Soda

3. Pemberton sold Coca-Cola to make people well and _____ their problems.
   a. keep   **b.** cure   **c.** mix

4. A medicine that cures many things is _____ .
   a. popular   **b.** all-purpose   **c.** free

5. The different things that are mixed together to make Coca-Cola are its _____ .
   a. ingredients   **b.** ideas   **c.** sodas

6. The _____ of ingredients is the amount you put in.
   a. factory   **b.** quantity   **c.** permission

7. Not many people knew about Pemberton's syrup. _____ bought it.
   a. A lot   **b.** Few   **c.** All

8. The way Coca-Cola's ingredients are put together is its _____ .
   a. ingredients   **b.** soda fountain   **c.** recipe

COMPREHENSION

A. Looking for Main Ideas

Write complete answers to these questions.

1. How was Coca-Cola first used?

   _____

2. What did Asa Candler sell Coca-Cola as?

   _____

3. When did Coca-Cola begin to become popular around the world?

   _____

B. Looking for Details

Number the sentences 1 through 8 to show the correct order.

_____ Today, there are Coca-Cola factories around the world.

_____ Few people bought John Pemberton's syrup.

_____ Asa Candler made Coca-Cola into a soda.

_____ That was how Coca-Cola became so popular in the United States.

_____ John Pemberton sold the recipe to Asa Candler.

_____ During World War I, the Coca-Cola Company sent Coca-Cola to U.S. soldiers in Europe.

_____ But two other businessmen put Coca-Cola into bottles.

_____ A druggist, John Pemberton, invented Coca-Cola in 1886.

GRAMMAR

Complete the sentences using the past tense form of the verbs in parentheses.

EXAMPLE: John Pemberton _____*was*_____ a druggist in Atlanta, Georgia.
                                      (be)

1. John Pemberton _____ a brown syrup.
                        (make)

2. He _____ this all-purpose medicine "Coca-Cola."
        (call)

3. Few people _____ it.
   (buy)

4. He _____ it to Asa Candler.
   (sell)

5. Candler _____ it with soda water.
   (mix)

6. Two other men _____ permission from Candler to put Coca-Cola
   (get)

   in bottles.

DISCUSSION

Discuss the answers to these questions with your classmates.

1. Why do people drink soft drinks? Do you think soft drinks are good for you?

2. Why do you think Coca-Cola is so popular around the world?

3. Describe a drink that is special to your country.

WRITING

Write six sentences or a short paragraph about how you prepare tea, coffee, or another drink. If you write a paragraph, be sure to indent the first sentence.

EXAMPLE: _In my country, Turkey, we make Turkish coffee. To make_
Turkish coffee you need very fine ground coffee, water,
sugar, and a "cezve," a special pot to cook the coffee.

THE HAMBURGER

PREREADING

Name all the things you can get on a hamburger.

The hamburger has no connection to ham. It got its name from the German town of Hamburg, which was famous for its ground steak. German immigrants to the United States introduced the "hamburger steak."

At the St. Louis World's Fair in 1904, hamburger steaks were served on buns for the first time. Hamburgers on buns were convenient and tasted good. This became the usual way of eating hamburgers.

How did the hamburger become the most popular, most typical American food? The introduction of the bun is an important part of the answer. Another important part is McDonald's, the fast-food restaurant.

The first McDonald's was opened in San Bernadino, California, in 1949. Hamburgers were the main item on its menu. People liked the restaurant's fast service. By the 1960s, there were many McDonald's restaurants. McDonald's was a part of nearly every community in the United States. There were also other fast-food restaurants that sold hamburgers. McDonald's alone sold millions of hamburgers a year.

Today, of course, there are McDonald's restaurants around the world. The food they serve is considered typically American. And, although McDonald's has expanded its menu, the main item on that menu is—as always—the hamburger.

VOCABULARY

Complete the sentences with one of the following words.

buns	typical	introduction
connection	community	convenient

1. The hamburger is not a type of ham. It has no _____ to ham.

2. Americans first put hamburgers on small, round pieces of bread,

   or _____ .

3. Eating hamburgers on buns is quick and easy. In other words, it's

   _____ .

4. The hamburger is one of the most _____ American foods.

5. The _____ of the bun helped the hamburger become popular.

6. Nearly every city or town in the United States has a McDonald's to serve the

   _____ .

COMPREHENSION

A. Looking for Main Ideas

Circle the letter of the best answer.

1. The hamburger was _____ .
   a. steak imported from Hamburg
   b. a ground steak introduced by immigrants
   c. a convenient bun

2. The American hamburger was different because it _____ .
   a. had nothing to do with ham
   b. was convenient
   c. was served on a bun

3. McDonald's restaurants were partly responsible for _____ .

    a. every community in the United States

    b. the introduction of the bun

    c. the hamburger's popularity

B. Looking for Details

Write complete answers to these questions.

1. Who introduced the hamburger to the United States?

_____

2. Where was the 1904 World's Fair?

_____

3. How do most people eat hamburgers?

_____

4. What do most people eat at McDonald's?

_____

5. What do you call convenience foods like hamburgers?

_____

6. Why is the hamburger considered a typical American food?

_____

GRAMMAR

Complete the sentences with the prepositions below.

of	on	at	for	By	in	to

EXAMPLE: The hamburger got its name __from__ the city of Hamburg.

    1. The hamburger has no connection _____ ham.

    2. Hamburg was famous _____ its ground steak.

    3. Hamburgers _____ buns were introduced _____ the World's Fair.

4. This is the usual way _____ eating hamburgers.

5. Hamburgers were the main item _____ the menu.

6. McDonald's is part _____ nearly every community _____ the United States.

7. _____ the 1960s, there were many McDonald's restaurants.

DISCUSSION

Discuss the answers to these questions with your classmates.

1. What types of fast food can you buy?

2. What are the advantages and disadvantages of fast food?

3. What do you think some fast foods of the future might be?

WRITING

Write six sentences or a short paragraph about the most popular dish in your country. What is it made of? When do people eat it? If you write a paragraph, be sure to indent the first sentence.

EXAMPLE: _A popular dish in my country, Korea, is kim-chi. We eat_ _kim-chi every day._

JAZZ

Unit 23

PREREADING

Name as many different kinds of music as you can.

Americans have contributed to many art forms, but jazz, a type of music, is the only art form that was created in the United States. Jazz was created by black Americans. Many blacks were brought from Africa to America as slaves. The black slaves sang and played the music of their homeland.

Jazz is a mixture of many different kinds of music. It is a combination of the music of West Africa, the work songs the slaves sang, and religious music. Improvisation is an important part of jazz. This means that the musicians make the music up as they go along, or create the music on the spot. This is why a jazz song might sound a little different each time it is played.

Jazz bands formed in the late 1800s. They played in bars and clubs in many towns and cities of the South, especially New Orleans.

New Orleans is an international seaport, and people from all over the world come to New Orleans to hear jazz.

Jazz became more and more popular. By the 1920s, jazz was popular all over the United States. By the 1940s, you could hear jazz not only in clubs and bars, but in concert halls as well. Today, people from all over the world play jazz. Jazz musicians from the United States, Asia, Africa, South America, and Europe meet and share their music at festivals on every continent. In this way jazz continues to grow and change.

VOCABULARY

Complete the sentences. Circle the letter of the correct answer.

1. Americans were the first to perform jazz music. It was _____ in the United States.
   a. contributed
   b. created

2. Many ships come to New Orleans because it is a big _____ .
   a. seaport
   b. continent

3. The black slaves sang and played the music of the place they were born. West Africa was their _____ .
   a. combination
   b. homeland

4. When you join with others and give ideas to create something, you _____ to it.
   a. improvise
   b. contribute

5. Jazz musicians from all over the world meet at _____ to play and share their music.
   a. festivals
   b. concert halls

6. Jazz musicians create music as they go along. They invent music _____ .
   a. to grow and change
   b. on the spot

COMPREHENSION

A. Looking for Main Ideas

Write complete answers to these questions.

1. What is jazz?

   _____

2. When did jazz become popular in the United States?

   _____

3. Who plays jazz today?

   _____

B. Looking for Details

One word in each sentence is *not* correct. Cross out the word and write the correct answer above it.

1. Blacks were brought to Africa as slaves.

2. They sang the music of their bands.

3. Jazz festivals formed in the late 1800s.

4. West Africa is an international seaport.

5. Improvisation is an important spot of jazz.

6. Jazz became popular all over the continent.

GRAMMAR

Complete the sentences using the correct tense of the verb in parentheses. Use either the simple present or the simple past.

EXAMPLE: Jazz _____*was*_____ created by black Americans.
                            (be)

1. Today, jazz _____ to grow and change.
                     (continue)

2. Jazz _____ more and more popular.
            (become)

3. The black slaves _____ and _____ the music of their
                          (sing)   (play)

   homeland.

4. A jazz song _____ different each time it is played.
     (sound)

5. Today, people from all over the world _____ jazz.
     (play)

6. Jazz _____ a mixture of different kinds of music.
     (be)

DISCUSSION

Discuss the answers to these questions with your classmates.

1. What musical instruments are played in jazz bands?

2. What music is special to your country?

3. Who is your favorite musician or singer?

WRITING

Write six sentences or a short paragraph about the music you like. If you write a paragraph, be sure to indent the first sentence.

EXAMPLE: My favorite kind of music is classical music. My favorite
              composer is Mozart.

_____

_____

BASEBALL

Unit 24

PREREADING

Name some sports you can play with a ball.

Baseball is the most popular sport in America. In a baseball game there are two teams of nine players. Players must hit a ball with a bat and then run around four bases. A player who goes around all the bases scores a run for his team. The team that finishes with more runs wins the game.

Where did baseball come from? No one knows for sure. Many people believe that the idea came from a game played by children in England. Other people believe that a man named Abner Doubleday invented the game in Cooperstown, New York, in 1839. But the first real rules of baseball were written in 1845 by Alexander Cartwright. Two teams from New York played a game following Cartwright's rules. The rules worked well. Soon there were many teams.

These early teams were not professional. They played only for fun, not money. But baseball was very popular from the start. Businessmen saw that they could make money with professional baseball teams.

The first professional team was started in 1869. This team was the Red Stockings of Cincinnati. Within a few years, there were professional teams in other cities. In 1876 these teams came together in a league, or group, called the National League. The teams in the National League played one another.

In 1901 a new league, called the American League, was formed. To create some excitement, in 1903 the two leagues decided to have their first-place teams play each other. This event was called the World Series.

Each year since then the National League winner and the American League winner play in the World Series. And, each year, millions of people look forward to this exciting sports event.

VOCABULARY

Complete the definitions. Circle the letter of the correct answer.

1. A group of people that play together is a _____ .
   a. team   **b.** league   **c.** game

2. A wooden stick used to hit a ball in baseball is called a _____ .
   a. ball   **b.** sport   **c.** bat

3. The four stations the players must go around are _____ .
   a. rules   **b.** bases   **c.** wins

4. When a player runs around all four bases, he makes a _____ .
   a. four   **b.** winner   **c.** run

5. Teams that play a game the correct way are following the _____ .
   a. runs   **b.** rules   **c.** players

6. A group of sports teams is called _____ .
   a. first-place teams   **b.** a league   **c.** a series

7. When something special or important happens, it is _____ .
   a. an event   **b.** popular   **c.** a series

8. When teams play sports for money, they are _____ .
   a. businessmen   **b.** fun   **c.** professional

COMPREHENSION

A. Looking for Main Ideas

Write the questions to these answers.

1. Where _____?

   No one knows where baseball came from. But the rules were written by Alexander Cartwright in 1845.

2. When _____?

   The first professional team started in 1869.

3. Who _____?

   The National League winner and the American League winner play in the World Series.

B. Looking for Details

Circle T if the sentence is true. Circle F if the sentence is false.

	True	False
1. Baseball was invented in England.	T	F
2. Abner Doubleday played the game with Alexander Cartwright.	T	F
3. The early teams played for fun.	T	F
4. The Red Stockings were the first professional team.	T	F
5. In 1876 nonprofessional teams came together in a league.	T	F
6. The World Series has been played since 1903.	T	F
7. Baseball players must hit a ball with a bat and run around nine bases.	T	F
8. The winning teams in each league play each other in the World Series.	T	F

GRAMMAR

Complete the sentences with the correct article. Use *a* or *the.* If no article is necessary, write *X.*

EXAMPLE: In __*a*__ baseball game there are __X__ two teams

of nine players.

1. _____ baseball is _____ America's most popular sport.

2. Players must hit _____ ball with _____ bat.

3. No one knows where _____ baseball came from.

4. Some people believe that _____ man named Abner Doubleday invented _____ game in _____ New York.

5. _____ businessmen saw they could make _____ money with professional teams.

6. The teams in _____ National League played one another.

7. In 1901 _____ American League was formed.

8. _____ National League winner and _____ American League winner play each other in _____ World Series.

DISCUSSION

Discuss the answers to these questions with your classmates.

1. Do you like sports? Why or why not?

2. What is the most popular sport in your country? Why do you think this sport is so popular? Do you think the people in your country should pay more or less attention to sports?

3. If you could be a professional athlete, which sport would you play and why?

WRITING

Write six sentences or a short paragraph. Describe a sport you like to watch or play. If you write a paragraph, be sure to indent the first sentence.

EXAMPLE: _A sport I like is ice-skating. I cannot ice-skate, but I like to watch skating on television._

_____

_____

UNCLE SAM

Unit 25

PREREADING

Name some symbols of countries you know.

Country	Symbol
Thailand	elephant

Uncle Sam is a tall, thin man. He's an older man with white hair and a white beard. He often wears a tall hat, a bow tie, and the stars and stripes of the American flag.

Who is this strange-looking man? Would you believe that Uncle Sam is the U.S. government? But why do we call the U.S. government Uncle Sam?

During the War of 1812, the U.S. government hired meat packers to provide meat to the army. One of these meat packers was a man named Samuel Wilson. He was a friendly and fair man. Everyone liked him and called him Uncle Sam.

Sam Wilson stamped the boxes of meat for the army with a large *U.S.*—for *United States.* Some government inspectors came to look over Wilson's company. They asked a worker what the *U.S.* on the boxes stood for. As a joke, the worker answered that these letters stood for the name of his boss, Uncle Sam.

The joke spread, and soldiers began saying that their food came from Uncle Sam. Before long, people called all things that came from the government "Uncle Sam's." "Uncle Sam" became a nickname for the U.S. government.

Soon there were drawings and cartoons of Uncle Sam in newspapers. In these early pictures, Uncle Sam was a young man. He wore stars and stripes, but his hair was dark and he had no beard. The beard was added when Abraham Lincoln was president. President Lincoln had a beard.

The most famous picture of Uncle Sam is on a poster from World War I. The government needed men to fight in the war. In the poster, a very serious Uncle Sam points his finger and says, "I want YOU for the U.S. Army."

VOCABULARY

Complete the sentences. Circle the letter of the correct answer.

1. The *U.S.* on the boxes _____ *United States*.
   - **a.** stamped
   - **b.** stood for
   - **c.** named

2. "Uncle Sam" became a _____ for the U.S. government.
   - **a.** boss
   - **b.** nickname
   - **c.** picture

3. There's a famous picture of Uncle Sam on a _____ from World War I.
   - **a.** joke
   - **b.** box
   - **c.** poster

4. Samuel Wilson was a friendly and _____ man.
   - **a.** fair
   - **b.** strange
   - **c.** young

5. The U.S. government _____ meat packers.
   - **a.** liked
   - **b.** hired
   - **c.** called

6. Uncle Sam often wears a tall hat, _____, and the stars and stripes of the American flag.
   - **a.** dark hair
   - **b.** a bow tie
   - **c.** a box

7. Government inspectors came to _____ Samuel Wilson's meat-packing company.
   - **a.** ask
   - **b.** stand for
   - **c.** look over

8. Samuel Wilson was a meat packer who _____ meat to the army.
   - **a.** provided
   - **b.** needed
   - **c.** added

COMPREHENSION

A. Looking for Main Ideas

Circle the letter of the best answer.

1. Everyone called Samuel Wilson _____ .
   a. Uncle Sam
   b. a joke
   c. the United States

2. Uncle Sam is _____ .
   a. the U.S. government
   b. the government meat packers
   c. the name of a government inspector

3. The most famous picture of Uncle Sam is _____ .
   a. on a poster from World War I
   b. in a newspaper from World War I
   c. when he was in the army in World War I

4. In the drawings and cartoons of Uncle Sam, he _____ .
   a. wore the stars and stripes
   b. never had a beard
   c. had no hair

B. Looking for Details

Circle T if the sentence is true. Circle F if the sentence is false.

	True	False
1. Uncle Sam is short and thin.	T	F
2. Sam Wilson was a meat packer.	T	F
3. Everyone liked Sam Wilson.	T	F
4. Sam Wilson stamped the boxes "Uncle Sam."	T	F
5. The government inspectors asked Samuel Wilson what the *U.S.* on the boxes stood for.	T	F
6. "Uncle Sam" became a nickname for President Lincoln.	T	F

GRAMMAR

Complete the sentences with the prepositions below.

with	of	on	in	for

EXAMPLE: Uncle Sam wears the stars and stripes ___of___ the American flag.

1. Uncle Sam is tall and thin _____ white hair and a beard.

2. Sam Wilson stamped the boxes _____ meat _____ the army.

3. The *U.S.* _____ the boxes stood for *United States*.

4. "Uncle Sam" became a nickname _____ the U.S. government.

5. There were drawings _____ Uncle Sam _____ newspapers.

6. Uncle Sam was a young man _____ these early pictures.

7. The most famous picture _____ Uncle Sam is _____ a poster from World War I.

8. The government needed men to fight _____ the war.

DISCUSSION

Discuss the answers to these questions with your classmates.

1. What are other symbols that represent the United States?

2. What other world symbols do you know?

3. How would you dress today's version of Uncle Sam?

WRITING

Write six sentences or a short paragraph about a famous world or country symbol. If you write a paragraph, be sure to indent the first sentence.

EXAMPLE: The symbol of Thailand is the elephant. The shape of our country is like the shape of an elephant's head.

_____

_____

THE GOLD RUSH

Unit 26

PREREADING

What expressions do you have in your language that use the word "gold"? Translate them into English.

It was January 1848. A man was digging near the small village of San Francisco, California. Suddenly, he saw something shiny—gold!

By the next year, the California gold rush had begun. Thousands of men came to California. They were called "forty-niners," after the year 1849. The forty-niners came from all around the United States. They even came from other countries, including Mexico, Australia, China, France, and England. They left their families and jobs and made the difficult trip to California. They all shared a dream. They all wanted to make a fortune in gold.

Towns and camps grew quickly wherever gold was found. These towns were rough places. There was almost always a saloon, where the men drank whiskey and gambled at cards. In mining towns, men stole and sometimes killed for gold.

Did the miners make their fortunes? Some did, especially those who came early and were lucky. In 1848, miners usually made about twenty dollars a day. In 1852, miners made about six dollars a day. Many other people came to California to make money from the miners. Prices were very high. A loaf of bread, which cost five cents in New York, cost almost a dollar in San Francisco.

In 1848, San Francisco had been a village. Six years later, it was a city with a population of 50,000. In 1850, California had enough people to become a state.

VOCABULARY

What is the meaning of the underlined words? Circle the letter of the correct answer.

1. They all wanted to <u>make a fortune</u> in gold.
   a. make a lot of time
   b. make a lot of money

2. The forty-niners all <u>shared a dream</u>.
   a. had the same dream
   b. wanted a different dream

3. The towns of the Old West were <u>rough places</u>.
   a. places where people fight a lot
   b. places where there are mountains

4. There were many <u>saloons</u> in these western towns.
   a. places to go to drink liquor
   b. places to go to find gold

5. Men <u>gambled at cards</u> in the saloons, too.
   a. played cards to get money
   b. played cards to have fun

6. Some men <u>stole</u> to get gold.
   a. paid for things that other people were selling
   b. took things that belonged to other people

COMPREHENSION

A. Looking for Main Ideas

Circle the letter of the best answer.

1. In 1849, thousands of men came to California because they _____ .
   - **a.** were forty-niners
   - **b.** wanted to find gold
   - **c.** had families

2. Towns and camps grew _____ .
   - **a.** quickly
   - **b.** where there was a saloon
   - **c.** where there was no gold

3. Some of the miners who were lucky made _____ .
   - **a.** twenty dollars
   - **b.** their fortune
   - **c.** bread

4. In 1850, California _____ .
   - **a.** had a population of 50,000
   - **b.** became a state
   - **c.** had only one village

B. Looking for Details

One word in each sentence is *not* correct. Cross out the word and write the correct answer above it.

1. In 1848, a miner made two dollars a day.

2. A loaf of bread cost five cents in England.

3. In 1854, San Francisco had a population of 500,000.

4. Some of the miners who came late were lucky.

5. Men gambled at whiskey in the saloons.

6. The forty-niners took their families and made the difficult trip to California.

GRAMMAR

Combine the two sentences into one using *and.*

EXAMPLE: Towns grew quickly wherever gold was found. Camps grew quickly wherever gold was found.

Towns and camps grew quickly wherever gold was found.

1. They left their families. They made the difficult trip to California.

2. In the saloons, the men drank whiskey. The men gambled at cards.

3. In the mining towns, men stole for gold. Men sometimes killed for gold.

4. Some of the miners who were early made their fortunes. Some of the miners who were lucky made their fortunes.

5. The forty-niners came from all around the United States. The forty-niners came from other countries.

DISCUSSION

Discuss the answers to these questions with your classmates.

1. Gold is used as a symbol of value. It also has some practical uses. How is it used in your country?

2. Are there any legends or stories about gold in your country's history? Tell the class.

3. Do people still value gold today? What other things do people consider of material value?

WRITING

Write six sentences or a short paragraph. What things have the greatest value for you? If you write a paragraph, be sure to indent the first sentence.

EXAMPLE: _It is nice to have a beautiful house and an expensive car. But the thing that has the greatest value for me is my family._

THE BALD EAGLE

Unit 27

PREREADING

Some people associate certain characteristics with certain animals. Name some animals and the characteristics you associate with them.

Animal	Association
lion	courage

In 1782, soon after the United States won its independence, the bald eagle was chosen as the national bird of the new country. American leaders wanted the eagle to be a symbol of their country because it is a bird of strength and courage. They chose the bald eagle because it was found all over North America and only in North America.

But a little over 200 years later, the bald eagle had almost disappeared from the country. In 1972, there were only 3,000 bald eagles in the entire United States.

The reason for the bird's decreasing population was pollution, especially pollution of the rivers by pesticides. Pesticides are chemicals used to kill insects and other animals that attack and destroy crops. Unfortunately, rain often washes pesticides into rivers. Pesticides pollute the rivers and poison the fish. Eagles eat these fish and the poison affects their eggs. The eggs have very thin shells and do not hatch. Eagles lay only two or three eggs a year. Because many of the eggs did not hatch and produce more eagles, the number of eagles quickly became smaller.

Today, the American government and the American people are trying to protect the bald eagle. The number of bald eagles is increasing. It now appears that the American national bird will survive and remain a symbol of strength and courage.

VOCABULARY

What is the meaning of the underlined words? Circle the letter of the correct answer.

1. In 1972, there were only 3,000 bald eagles in the <u>entire</u> United States.
   a. whole   **b.** central

2. The reason for the bird's decreasing population was <u>pollution</u>.
   a. other animals   **b.** dirty air and water

3. The eggs have thin shells and do not <u>hatch</u>.
   a. open   **b.** fly

4. Eagles <u>lay</u> only two or three eggs a year.
   a. eat   **b.** produce

5. Pesticides kill animals that attack and destroy <u>crops</u>.
   a. insects   **b.** plants

6. It now appears that the American national bird will <u>survive</u>.
   a. live   **b.** die

COMPREHENSION

A. Looking for Main Ideas

Write complete answers to these questions.

1. Why was the bald eagle chosen as the symbol of the United States?

   _____

2. Why did the bald eagle almost disappear from the country?

   _____

3. What are the American government and the American people trying to do for the bald eagle?

   _____

B. Looking for Details

One **word in each sentence is** *not* **correct. Cross out the word and write the correct answer above it.**

1. The United States won its independence after 1782.

2. American leaders wanted the eagle to be a sample of their country.

3. They chose the bald eagle because it was found all over South America.

4. A little over 200 years late, the bald eagle had almost disappeared.

5. In 1972, there were only 30,000 bald eagles.

6. Unfortunately, rain often washes crops into rivers.

7. The eagles have very thin shells and do not hatch.

8. Today, the American government and the American people are trying to pollute the bald eagle.

GRAMMAR

Complete the sentences with the article *the.* **If no article is necessary, write X.**

EXAMPLE: __The__ bald eagle almost disappeared from __the__ country.

1. They chose _____ bald eagle because it was found all over North America.

2. The reason for _____ bird's decreasing population was _____ pollution.

3. _____ pesticides are _____ chemicals used to kill _____ insects.

4. _____ eagles eat the poisoned fish.

5. Because many of _____ eggs did not hatch and produce more _____ eagles, _____ number of _____ eagles became smaller.

6. Today, _____ American government and _____ American people are trying to protect _____ bald eagle.

DISCUSSION

Discuss the answers to these questions with your classmates.

1. Which animals are closely associated with your country?

2. If you could be an animal, what animal would you be? Why?

3. How are some animals useful to people?

WRITING

Write a short paragraph telling a story about an animal. Be sure to indent the first sentence.

EXAMPLE: One day a cat attacked one of our chickens. But the chicken was not dead. My mother took care of the chicken.

_____

_____

TORNADOES

Unit 28

PREREADING

What do you know about tornadoes? Circle T or F.

		True	False
1.	Tornadoes are the strongest winds.	T	F
2.	Tornadoes are common all over the world.	T	F
3.	Tornadoes occur in the winter.	T	F
4.	People don't die in tornadoes.	T	F
5.	People cannot stop tornadoes.	T	F
6.	Tornadoes last for several days.	T	F

Tornadoes are storms with very strong turning winds and dark clouds. These winds are perhaps the strongest on earth. They reach speeds of 300 miles per hour. The dark clouds are shaped like a funnel—wide at the top and narrow at the bottom. The winds are strongest in the center of the funnel.

Tornadoes are especially common in the United States, but only in certain parts. They occur mainly in the central states.

A hot afternoon in the spring is the most likely time for a tornado. Clouds become dark. There is thunder, lightning, and rain. A cloud forms a funnel and begins to twist. The funnel moves faster and faster. The faster the winds, the louder the noise. Tornadoes always move in a northeastern direction. They never last longer than eight hours.

A tornado's path is narrow, but within that narrow path, a tornado can destroy everything. It can smash buildings and rip up trees. Tornadoes can kill people as well.

The worst tornado swept through the states of Missouri, Illinois, and Indiana in 1925, killing 689 people. Modern weather equipment now makes it possible to warn people of tornadoes. People have a much better chance of protecting themselves. But nothing can stop tornadoes from destroying everything in their path.

VOCABULARY

Replace the underlined words in the sentences with the words below.

a funnel	warned	rip up	path
likely	swept	twist	occur

1. A tornado has the shape of <u>something that is wide at the top and narrow at the bottom</u>.

2. A tornado is so strong that it can <u>pull up</u> trees.

3. The most <u>probable</u> time for a tornado is on a hot afternoon in spring.

4. The worst tornado <u>moved quickly and powerfully</u> through Missouri in 1925, killing many people.

5. A cloud forms a funnel and it begins to <u>turn</u>.

6. With modern weather equipment people can be <u>told of something bad before it happens</u>.

7. A tornado has a narrow <u>line along which it moves</u>.

8. In the United States, tornadoes <u>happen</u> mainly in the central states.

COMPREHENSION

A. Looking for Main Ideas

Write the questions to these answers.

1. What _____?
   They are storms with very strong winds and dark clouds.

2. Where _____?
   They are especially common in the central states of the United
   States.

3. When _____?
   The most likely time for a tornado is a hot afternoon in spring.

B. Looking for Details

One word in each sentence is not correct. Cross out the word and write the correct answer above it.

1. The winds are strongest in the center of the earth.

2. A tornado always moves in a southeastern direction.

3. A tornado cannot kill people.

4. A tornado never lasts longer than eight days.

5. A tornado can reach speeds of 689 miles per hour.

6. Equipment can stop tornadoes from destroying everything in their path.

7. Clouds become hot in a tornado.

8. A tornado can kill buildings and rip up trees.

GRAMMAR

Combine the two sentences into one using and or but.

EXAMPLE: Tornadoes are storms with strong turning winds.
Tornadoes are storms with dark clouds.

Tornadoes are storms with strong turning winds
and dark clouds.

1. The dark clouds are wide at the top. The dark clouds are narrow at the bottom.

2. Tornadoes are common in the United States. They are common only in certain parts of the United States.

3. A cloud forms a funnel. A cloud begins to twist.

4. A tornado's path is narrow. Within that narrow path, it can destroy everything.

5. A tornado can smash buildings. A tornado can rip up trees.

DISCUSSION

Discuss the answers to these questions with your classmates.

1. What other types of natural disasters can you name?

2. How can you prepare for natural disasters?

3. Why do you think people rebuild in places where natural disasters occur?

WRITING

Write six sentences or a short paragraph about a natural disaster you have seen or heard about. If you write a paragraph, be sure to indent the first sentence.

EXAMPLE: A few years ago, there was an earthquake in Los Angeles.

I was there at that time.

_____

_____

THE JOSHUA TREE

Unit 29

Name some plants that are useful to people. Say how they are useful.

In the 1840s, the Mormons, who are a religious group, traveled west searching for a new home. Many Mormons lived in the state of Illinois. But they had been badly treated and finally were forced to leave. As the Mormons traveled through the desert, they became discouraged. Then they saw a strange tree. The tree's branches stretched out like arms. The Mormons thought the tree looked like Joshua, a hero from the Bible. The Mormons thought the arms of the tree were telling them to continue on their way, so they did. They found a new home in what is now the state of Utah. In Utah they saw trees like the one in the desert. They called them "Joshua trees."

The Joshua tree was very useful. The Native Americans of the West used almost all its parts. They ate not only the fruit of the tree, but also its seeds and white blossoms. They used its leaves for shoes. From its roots they made baskets and got colors for their clothes.

Settlers in the West used the Joshua tree for firewood and fences. Unfortunately, they often needed to cut down the trees. Some of the trees were as tall as fifty feet. These trees were 700 or 800 years old. The Joshua tree grows very slowly. It grows only about one inch a year.

By the beginning of the 1900s, most Joshua trees had been cut down. People were sad that this strange tree had almost disappeared.

In 1936, the Joshua Tree National Monument was established in California. It has many kinds of interesting desert plants, including, of course, many Joshua trees. None of these Joshua trees are fifty feet. But perhaps someday they will be.

VOCABULARY

Which sentences have the same meaning as the sentences from the reading? Circle the letter of the correct answer.

1. The Mormons traveled west searching for a new home.
   a. They were leaving their new home.
   b. They were looking for a new home.

2. The Mormons had been badly treated in Illinois.
   a. Other people in Illinois acted badly toward the Mormons.
   b. Other people in Illinois gave the Mormons gifts.

3. The Mormons became discouraged as they traveled through the desert.
   a. They felt very tired as they traveled through the desert.
   b. They didn't have much hope that they would find a new home.

4. They saw a strange tree.
   a. The tree they saw was unusual.
   b. The tree they saw was useful.

5. Joshua was a hero from the Bible.
   a. There are stories in the Bible about an old man named Joshua.
   b. There are stories in the Bible about a great man named Joshua.

6. The Native Americans ate not only the fruit of the tree, but also its seeds and white blossoms.
   a. The Native Americans ate the seeds and the flowers, but not the fruit.
   b. The Native Americans ate the seeds, flowers, and fruit.

COMPREHENSION

A. Looking for Main Ideas

Write the questions to these answers.

1. Where _____?
   The Mormons traveled west in search of a new home.

2. Who _____?
   They thought the tree looked like Joshua, a hero from the Bible.

3. What _____?
   The Native Americans used almost all parts of the tree.

B. Looking for Details

One word in each sentence is *not* correct. Cross out the word and write the correct answer above it.

1. The Native Americans of the West made shoes from the roots of the Joshua tree.

2. Some of the trees the settlers cut down were 700 feet tall.

3. In Illinois the Mormons saw trees like the one in the desert.

4. The Mormons were asked to leave Illinois.

5. The Joshua tree grows one foot a year.

6. In 1936, the Joshua Tree National Monument in Utah was established.

GRAMMAR

Complete the sentences using the correct tense of the verbs in parentheses. Use either the simple present or the simple past.

EXAMPLE: The Mormons ___*became*___ discouraged.
(become)

1. In the 1840s, the Mormons _____ west.
   (travel)

2. The Mormons _____ a religious group.
   (be)

3. The Joshua Tree National Monument _____ many kinds of desert plants.
   (have)

4. The Mormons _____ the tree looked like Joshua.
(think)

5. The Mormons _____ a new home in the state of Utah.
(find)

6. The Joshua tree _____ very slowly.
(grow)

DISCUSSION

Discuss the answers to these questions with your classmates.

1. The Joshua tree was used for many things. What other things can be made from trees?

2. The Joshua tree helped the Mormons and the Native Americans survive in the desert. How would you survive in the desert?

3. The Joshua tree almost disappeared. What problems are there with the forests of the world today?

WRITING

Write six sentences or a short paragraph about a plant useful to people. If you write a paragraph, be sure to indent the first sentence.

EXAMPLE: Bamboo is a very useful plant. People use bamboo stems to build houses and make pipes for water to go through.

_____

_____

SKUNKS, RACCOONS, AND COYOTES

Unit 30

PREREADING

Match the animal with what is special about it.

1. The snake   **a.** is a bird that cannot fly.

2. The giraffe   **b.** runs very fast.

3. The penguin   **c.** can eat an animal bigger than its body.

4. The cheetah   **d.** is the tallest animal.

5. The monkey   **e.** is the biggest land animal.

6. The elephant   **f.** hangs from trees with its tail.

THE SKUNK

The skunk is known mainly for its bad smell. Skunks are black and white and very furry. They are small—no larger than house cats.

When a skunk is in danger, it attacks by spraying a liquid from under its tail. This liquid has a terrible smell, which may last for many days. A skunk can spray something from as far away as twelve feet.

THE RACCOON

The raccoon is famous for its ringed tail and for the black "mask" around its eyes. Raccoons can use their paws skillfully and are quite intelligent. They eat many different things—frogs, fish, birds' eggs, fruit, and mice.

Raccoons are not timid or afraid of people. They'll often take food from garbage cans. This explains, some people say, the black masks around their eyes—raccoons are garbage-can robbers!

THE COYOTE

Coyotes are associated with the American Southwest. A coyote howling at night is a familiar scene in western movies. The coyote is a relative of the wolf. Like wolves, coyotes are not popular with farmers because they sometimes kill chickens and sheep. The coyote can live in many different kinds of places. Today, coyotes can be found all over the United States—from Alaska to New York and in towns as well as in the wild.

VOCABULARY

Which sentences have the same meaning as the sentences from the reading? Circle the letter of the correct answer.

1. Skunks are very furry.
   a. Skunks are very dangerous.
   b. Skunks have a lot of hair.

2. The raccoon is famous for its ringed tail.
   a. The raccoon is known for the black rings around its tail.
   b. The raccoon is known for its round tail.

3. Raccoons use their paws very skillfully.
   a. Raccoons use their heads cleverly.
   b. Raccoons are very good at using their hands and feet for many things.

4. Coyotes are associated with the American Southwest.
   a. When we think of the American Southwest, we think of coyotes.
   b. Coyotes can only live in the American Southwest.

5. A coyote howling at night is a familiar scene in western movies.
   a. It is common to see and hear a coyote making noise at night in a western movie.
   b. We often see cowboy movies with a coyote walking in the night.

COMPREHENSION

A. Looking for Main Ideas

Circle the letter of the best answer.

1. The skunk is known for _____ .
   a. its color
   b. its bad smell
   c. its fur

2. The raccoon is famous for _____ .
   a. the black "mask" around its eyes and its ringed tail
   b. eating mice and frogs
   c. its paws

3. The coyote is associated with _____ .
   a. the American Southwest
   b. the movies
   c. chickens and sheep

B. Looking for Details

One word in each sentence is not correct. Cross out the word and write the correct answer above it.

1. The skunk attacks by spraying a smell from under its tail.

2. The terrible smell may last for twelve days.

3. The coyote is a relative of the farmer.

4. Coyotes are not popular because they sometimes kill farmers.

5. Raccoons often take food from houses.

6. Skunks are black and white and very popular.

7. Skunks often take food from garbage cans.

8. Raccoons can spray their paws skillfully.

GRAMMAR

Complete the sentences with the prepositions below.

from	under	around	over	in	at	to

EXAMPLE: A raccoon has black rings ___around___ its tail.

1. A skunk sprays a liquid from _____ its tail.

2. A raccoon has a black "mask" _____ its eyes.

3. Raccoons often take food _____ garbage cans.

4. A coyote howling _____ night is a familiar scene _____ western movies.

5. Coyotes can be found all _____ the United States.

6. Coyotes can be found _____ Alaska _____ New York.

7. Coyotes can be found _____ towns as well as _____ the wild.

8. A skunk can spray something _____ twelve feet away.

DISCUSSION

Discuss the answers to these questions with your classmates.

1. What other animals live in North America?

2. What happens to wild animals when cities get bigger?

3. What things can we do to save animals that are becoming extinct?

WRITING

Write six sentences or a short paragraph about an animal you like or know. If you write a paragraph, be sure to indent the first sentence.

EXAMPLE: ___I like the dolphin. It is a very intelligent animal.___

_____

_____

ANSWER KEY

Unit 1

Vocabulary: **1.** b **2.** c **3.** a **4.** b **5.** b **6.** c **7.** a **8.** b

Looking for Main Ideas:
1. George Washington was chosen to lead the American army. **2.** People respected George Washington because he was a great leader and was not interested in fame or money, but only in helping his country. **3.** George Washington became the country's first president in 1789.

Looking for Details: **1.** F **2.** T **3.** T **4.** F **5.** F **6.** T **7.** T **8.** T

Grammar: **1.** knew **2.** was **3.** were, had **4.** thought **5.** attacked **6.** won **7.** met **8.** voted

Unit 2

Vocabulary: **1.** a **2.** a **3.** b **4.** a **5.** b **6.** b **7.** b **8.** a

Looking for Main Ideas:
1. Amelia Earhart was famous because she was the first woman pilot to fly across the United States. **2.** Amelia Earhart had great courage and ambition. **3.** Amelia Earhart's last flight is a mystery because to this day no one knows what happened to her, Fred Noonan, and the *Electra.*

Looking for Details: **1.** c **2.** b **3.** b **4.** c **5.** a **6.** a

Grammar: **1.** a **2.** the, the, a **3.** the, the, X, X **4.** X **5.** a **6.** X, X **7.** X **8.** the

Unit 3

Vocabulary: **1.** b **2.** c **3.** b **4.** a **5.** b **6.** c **7.** b **8.** c

Looking for Main Ideas:
1. Jesse Owens had athletic ability. **2.** Hitler wanted to show the world the Germans were the best. **3.** Jesse Owens won four gold medals at the 1936 Olympics.

Looking for Details: 3, 5, 1, 2, 7, 6, 4, 8

Grammar: **1.** X **2.** a, X **3.** the **4.** an **5.** the, the, the **6.** the **7.** the **8.** a

Unit 4

Vocabulary: **1.** the deaf **2.** wire **3.** fair **4.** an expert **5.** boardinghouse **6.** experiment **7.** attractions **8.** rushed

Looking for Main Ideas:
1. b **2.** c **3.** a

Looking for Details: **1.** T **2.** T **3.** F **4.** F **5.** F **6.** T

Grammar: **1.** in **2.** to **3.** in **4.** on, on **5.** through **6.** from, to

Unit 5

Prereading: 1, 2, 3, 6

Vocabulary: **1.** b **2.** c **3.** a **4.** c **5.** b **6.** c **7.** a **8.** b

Looking for Main Ideas:
1. When is Thanksgiving celebrated? **2.** Who were the Pilgrims? **3.** Why did the Pilgrims have a feast?

Looking for Details: 4, 7, 1, 6, 2, 5, 3, 8

Grammar: **1.** landed **2.** was **3.** died **4.** had **5.** taught **6.** invited

Unit 6

Vocabulary. **1.** b **2.** a **3.** b **4.** a **5.** a **6.** b **7.** b **8.** a

Looking for Main Ideas:
1. They use the "silent language" of gestures. **2.** It is important to know the body language of a country because we may be misunderstood if we don't know it. **3.** A person must not stand too close while talking to an American because Americans like to have space.

Looking for Details: **1.** b **2.** a **3.** b **4.** c

Grammar: **1.** of **2.** with **3.** on **4.** by **5.** in **6.** at

Unit 7

Prereading: **1.** T **2.** F **3.** F **4.** T **5.** T **6.** F

Vocabulary: **1.** a **2.** b **3.** a **4.** a **5.** b **6.** a **7.** b **8.** a

Looking for Main Ideas:
1. Levi Strauss came to California to sell canvas to the gold miners. **2.** The miners needed strong pants. **3.** He used a fabric called "denim," which was softer than canvas but just as strong.

Looking for Details:
1. ~~Germany~~/San Francisco **2.** ~~canvas~~/gold **3.** ~~buy~~/sell **4.** ~~clean~~/strong **5.** ~~tents~~/pants **6.** ~~Germany~~/France **7.** ~~red~~/blue **8.** ~~United States~~/world

Grammar: **1.** Miners **2.** Levi Strauss **3.** canvas **4.** pants **5.** the denim **6.** Levi Strauss

Unit 8

Prereading: 1, 2, 6, 7

Vocabulary: **1.** b **2.** a **3.** c **4.** b **5.** c **6.** b **7.** b **8.** b

Looking for Main Ideas:
1. a **2.** b **3.** b

Looking for Details:
1. ~~west~~/east **2.** ~~eight~~/sixteen **3.** ~~sixteen~~/eight **4.** ~~days~~/month **5.** ~~rustlers~~/cattle **6.** ~~rustlers~~/cattle **7.** ~~cowboys~~/beef **8.** ~~well~~/badly

Grammar: **1.** a **2.** the, X **3.** the, the, X **4.** the **5.** a **6.** X **7.** a **8.** X

Unit 9

Vocabulary: **1.** a **2.** b **3.** b **4.** a **5.** b **6.** a

Looking for Main Ideas: **1.** b **2.** a **3.** b

Looking for Details: **1.** T **2.** F **3.** F **4.** F **5.** T **6.** T

Grammar: **1.** The, X, a, the, the, X **2.** the, X, the, a **3.** X, X, the, X, X **4.** The, the **5.** The, the

Unit 10

Vocabulary: **1.** gangster **2.** gambling **3.** couple **4.** Neon **5.** license **6.** Casinos **7.** mispronunciation **8.** chapels

Looking for Main Ideas: **1.** Going into each hotel is like entering another world. **2.** Las Vegas is called the "City of Lights" and the "Diamond in the Desert" because it has so many neon lights. **3.** Las Vegas has more churches for its population than any other place in the United States.

Looking for Details: **1.** F **2.** F **3.** F **4.** T **5.** F **6.** T **7.** T

Grammar: **1.** for **2.** with **3.** from **4.** in **5.** to **6.** of

Unit 11

Prereading: **1.** T **2.** T **3.** F **4.** F **5.** T **6.** F

Vocabulary: **1.** b **2.** b **3.** b **4.** a **5.** b **6.** a

Looking for Main Ideas: **1.** The president of the United States lives in the White House. **2.** The White House was built in Washington because it was to be the nation's capital city. **3.** The original home of the president needed to be

rebuilt because it had burned down.

Looking for Details: **1.** b **2.** c **3.** b **4.** c **5.** c **6.** b

Grammar: **1.** The White House **2.** The British **3.** George Washington and Pierre-Charles L'Enfant **4.** Abigail Adams **5.** James Hoban **6.** White paint **7.** George Washington **8.** United States and Britain

Unit 12

Vocabulary: **1.** industry **2.** century **3.** scenery **4.** Nearly **5.** powerful **6.** glamorous **7.** autograph

Looking for Main Ideas: **1.** c **2.** b **3.** c

Looking for Details: **1.** T **2.** F **3.** T **4.** F **5.** T **6.** F

Grammar: **1.** to **2.** in **3.** at **4.** in **5.** in, in **6.** for **7.** from, to **8.** to

Unit 13

Vocabulary: **1.** b **2.** a **3.** a **4.** c **5.** b **6.** c **7.** a **8.** b

Looking for Main Ideas: **1.** a **2.** c **3.** a

Looking for Details: **1.** ~~zoos~~/ malls **2.** ~~expensive~~/free **3.** ~~smallest~~/largest **4.** ~~1948~~/ 1965 **5.** ~~gifts~~/food **6.** ~~friends~~/ exercise

Grammar: **1.** with **2.** in **3.** for **4.** from **5.** to **6.** In

Unit 14

Vocabulary: **1.** spoke out **2.** novel **3.** Slaves **4.** escape **5.** published **6.** causes

Looking for Main Ideas: **1.** b **2.** a **3.** a

Looking for Details: **1.** b **2.** a **3.** b **4.** b **5.** b

Grammar: **1.** *Uncle Tom's Cabin* was written by Harriet Beecher Stowe and was published in 1852. **2.** Slavery

had been abolished in the North, but most Northerners were willing to let slavery continue in the South. **3.** Harriet Beecher Stowe had six children and wrote every night after she put them to bed. **4.** People in the North agreed with *Uncle Tom's Cabin,* but people in the South were angry. **5.** Disagreements between North and South grew, and by 1861 there was war. **6.** The Civil War lasted until 1865 and brought an end to slavery.

Unit 15

Prereading: **1.** F **2.** T **3.** F **4.** T **5.** F **6.** T

Vocabulary: **1.** b **2.** a **3.** b **4.** c **5.** c **6.** a **7.** a **8.** b

Looking for Main Ideas: **1.** c **2.** b **3.** a

Looking for Details: 3, 7, 5, 1, 6, 2, 4

Grammar: **1.** admired **2.** survived **3.** won **4.** began **5.** gave **6.** started

Unit 16

Prereading: mouse, software, disk, keyboard, memory, monitor

Vocabulary: **1.** achieved **2.** get over **3.** giant **4.** dormitory **5.** obsession with **6.** will **7.** software **8.** dropped out of

Looking for Main Ideas: **1.** Where did Bill Gates meet his business partner? **2.** Why did Bill Gates and Paul Allen create Microsoft? **3.** How hard did Bill Gates work for more than ten years?

Looking for Details: **1.** b **2.** b **3.** c **4.** a **5.** b **6.** c

Grammar: **1.** Many people cannot imagine life without PCs, but PCs are actually a recent invention. **2.** In the eighth grade, Paul Allen and Bill Gates were writing programs for business computers and making money. **3.** Gates's parents wanted their son to become a lawyer, but he dropped out of Harvard two years later. **4.** Paul Allen recovered from cancer and started his own company. **5.** At the age of thirty-four, Bill Gates was a billionaire and the "King of Software." **6.** Bill Gates had a dream and the will to succeed.

Unit 17

Prereading: American English: color, honor, advertise, gray, surprise, check, program, center

Vocabulary: **1.** a **2.** b **3.** b **4.** c **5.** b

Looking for Main Ideas: **1.** He wrote a grammar book, a spelling book, and a reader. **2.** He wanted words to be spelled the way they were pronounced. **3.** His most famous work was the American English dictionary.

Looking for Details: **1.** T **2.** F **3.** T **4.** T **5.** F **6.** T **7.** F **8.** T

Grammar: **1.** Noah Webster **2.** American children **3.** The books **4.** spellings **5.** few words **6.** The British **7.** the money, his great work **8.** Webster's dictionary

Unit 18

Vocabulary: **1.** a **2.** a **3.** b **4.** b **5.** a

Looking for Main Ideas: **1.** c **2.** b **3.** a

Looking for Details: **1.** T **2.** F **3.** T **4.** F **5.** F **6.** T **7.** F **8.** T

Grammar: **1.** grew up **2.** left **3.** went **4.** built **5.** won **6.** cost **7.** bought **8.** sold

Unit 19

Vocabulary: **1.** b **2.** c **3.** a **4.** b **5.** a **6.** c

Looking for Main Ideas: **1.** What did Americans call frankfurters? **2.** Where in the United States were dachshund sausages first sold? **3.** Who was Tad Dorgan?

Looking for Details: **1.** F **2.** T **3.** F **4.** F **5.** F **6.** T

Grammar: **1.** became **2.** kept **3.** got **4.** went **5.** saw **6.** wrote

Unit 20

Prereading: **1.** F **2.** F **3.** T **4.** T **5.** T

Vocabulary: **1.** b **2.** a **3.** a **4.** a **5.** a **6.** b

Looking for Main Ideas: **1.** A cranberry is a North American fruit that grows on a bush. **2.** The cranberry bush grows in five states: Washington, Oregon, Wisconsin, Massachusetts, and New Jersey. **3.** John Webb developed the special method of separating the cranberries.

Looking for Details: **1.** ~~more~~/less **2.** ~~best~~/bad **3.** ~~method~~/step **4.** ~~Native Americans~~/settlers **5.** ~~Easter~~/Thanksgiving **6.** ~~cooled~~/cooked **7.** ~~summer~~/fall **8.** ~~easy~~/hard

Grammar: **1.** the, X **2.** The, the **3.** the **4.** X, the, the **5.** the, X, X **6.** a, a **7.** the, the **8.** a, a, X

Unit 21

Prereading: **1.** T **2.** F **3.** F **4.** T **5.** F **6.** T

Vocabulary: **1.** a **2.** a **3.** b **4.** b **5.** a **6.** b **7.** b **8.** c

Looking for Main Ideas: **1.** Coca-Cola was first used as a medicine. **2.** Asa Candler sold Coca-Cola as a soda-fountain drink. **3.** Coca-Cola began to become popular around the world during World War I.

Looking for Details: 8, 2, 4, 6, 3, 7, 5, 1

Grammar: **1.** made **2.** called **3.** bought **4.** sold **5.** mixed **6.** got

Unit 22

Vocabulary: **1.** connection **2.** buns **3.** convenient **4.** typical **5.** introduction **6.** community

Looking for Main Ideas: **1.** b **2.** c **3.** c

Looking for Details: **1.** German immigrants introduced the hamburger to the United States. **2.** The 1904 World's Fair was in St. Louis. **3.** The usual way of eating hamburgers is on a bun. **4.** The main menu item at McDonald's is the hamburger. **5.** Convenience-type food is called "fast" food. **6.** The hamburger is considered typically American because it is one of the most popular foods in the United States.

Grammar: **1.** to **2.** for **3.** on, at **4.** of **5.** on **6.** of, in **7.** By

Unit 23

Vocabulary: **1.** b **2.** a **3.** b **4.** b **5.** a **6.** b

Looking for Main Ideas: **1.** Jazz is a type of music. **2.** By the 1920s, jazz was popular all over the United States. **3.** People all over the world play jazz today.

Looking for Details: **1.** ~~Africa~~/America **2.** ~~bands~~/homeland **3.** ~~festivals~~/bands

4. ~~West Africa~~/New Orleans
5. ~~spot~~/part **6.** ~~continent~~/
world

Grammar: **1.** continues
2. became **3.** sang, played
4. sounds **5.** play **6.** is

Unit 24

Vocabulary: **1.** a **2.** c **3.** b
4. c **5.** b **6.** b **7.** a **8.** c

Looking for Main Ideas:
1. Where did baseball come
from? **2.** When did the first
professional team start?
3. Who plays in the World
Series?

Looking for Details: **1.** F
2. F **3.** T **4.** T **5.** F **6.** T **7.** F
8. T

Grammar: **1.** X, X **2.** the, a
3. X **4.** a, the, X **5.** X, X **6.** the
7. the **8.** The, the, the

Unit 25

Vocabulary: **1.** b **2.** b **3.** c
4. a **5.** b **6.** b **7.** c **8.** a

Looking for Main Ideas:
1. a **2.** a **3.** a **4.** a

Looking for Details: **1.** F **2.**
T **3.** T **4.** F **5.** F **6.** F

Grammar: **1.** with **2.** of, for
3. on **4.** for **5.** of, in **6.** in **7.**
of, on **8.** in

Unit 26

Vocabulary: **1.** b **2.** a **3.** a
4. a **5.** a **6.** b

Looking for Main Ideas:
1. b **2.** a **3.** b **4.** b

Looking for Details: **1.** ~~two~~/
twenty **2.** ~~England~~/New York
3. ~~500,000~~/50,000 **4.**
~~late~~/early
5. ~~whiskey~~/cards **6.** ~~took~~/left

Grammar: **1.** They left their
families and made the
difficult trip to California. **2.**
In the saloons, the men drank
whiskey and gambled at
cards. **3.** In the mining towns,
men stole and sometimes
killed for gold.

4. Some of the miners who
were early and lucky made
their fortunes. **5.** The forty-
niners came from all around
the United States and from
other countries.

Unit 27

Vocabulary: **1.** a **2.** b **3.** a
4. b **5.** b **6.** a

Looking for Main Ideas:
1. The bald eagle was chosen
as the symbol of the United
States because it is a bird of
strength and courage, and it
was found all over North
America. **2.** The bald eagle
almost disappeared from the
country because of pollution.
3. The American government
and the American people are
trying to protect the bald
eagle.

Looking for Details:
1. ~~after~~/before **2.** ~~sample~~/
symbol **3.** ~~South~~/North
4. ~~late~~/later **5.** ~~30,000~~/3,000
6. ~~crops~~/pesticides **7.** ~~eagles~~/
eggs **8.** ~~pollute~~/protect

Grammar: **1.** the **2.** the, X
3. X, X, X **4.** X **5.** the, X, the,
X **6.** the, the, the

Unit 28

Prereading: **1.** T **2.** F **3.** F
4. F **5.** T **6.** F

Vocabulary: **1.** a funnel **2.** rip
up **3.** likely **4.** swept **5.** twist
6. warned **7.** path **8.** occur

Looking for Main Ideas:
1. What are tornadoes?
2. Where are tornadoes
common in the United States?
3. When is the most likely
time for a tornado?

Looking for Details:
1. ~~earth~~/funnel
2. ~~southeastern~~/northeastern
3. ~~cannot~~/can **4.** ~~days~~/hours
5. ~~689~~/300 **6.** ~~Equipment~~/
Nothing **7.** ~~hot~~/dark
8. ~~kill~~/smash

Grammar: **1.** The dark
clouds are wide at the top and
narrow at the bottom. **2.**
Tornadoes are common in the
United States, but only in
certain parts. **3.** A cloud
forms a funnel and begins to
twist. **4.** A tornado's path is
narrow, but within that
narrow path it can destroy
everything. **5.** A tornado can
smash buildings and rip up
trees.

Unit 29

Vocabulary: **1.** b **2.** a **3.** b
4. a **5.** b **6.** b

Looking for Main Ideas:
1. Where did the Mormons
travel in search of a new
home? **2.** Who did they think
the tree looked like? **3.** What
parts of the tree did the
Native Americans use?

Looking for Details:
1. ~~shoes~~/baskets **2.** ~~700~~/fifty
3. ~~Illinois~~/Utah **4.** ~~asked~~/
forced **5.** ~~foot~~/inch **6.** ~~Utah~~/
California

Grammar: **1.** traveled **2.** are
3. has **4.** thought **5.** found
6. grows

Unit 30

Prereading: **1.** c **2.** d **3.** a
4. b **5.** f **6.** e

Vocabulary: **1.** b **2.** a **3.** b
4. a **5.** a

Looking for Main Ideas:
1. b **2.** a **3.** a

Looking for Details:
1. ~~smell~~/liquid **2.** ~~twelve~~/
many **3.** ~~farmer~~/wolf
4. ~~farmers~~/chickens and sheep
5. ~~houses~~/garbage cans
6. ~~popular~~/furry **7.** ~~Skunks~~/
Raccoons **8.** ~~spray~~/use

Grammar: **1.** under **2.**
around **3.** from **4.** at, in
5. over **6.** from, to **7.** in, in
8. from